Wilay

Wilay

Amor Vincit Omnia

Jeremy Limn

Published by Tablo

TABLE OF CONTENTS

PREFACE

Wilay is a collection of poems and micro-fiction that investigates the art of expressionism. Leonard Cohen said, "there is a crack in everything, that's how the light gets in." Poetry looks for the holes, in reality, the holes of inexperience. Wilay is a word from my native tongue, Wiradjuri. It means Possum, and so it is emblematic of this book. It is a dream-time theme that is a facet of everything this book has to offer.

Wilay is my dreaming it is my connection to the land and my Wiradjuri culture. The land is a part of me so you will see a lot of poems, and stories about the land, and nature.

To me, the stanza is a valley, and a stanza objectively is everything, lyrically. Poetry is merely an innate power that is installed within everybody and everything. William Blake tapped into this power through the roots of Christianity. His focus is on the livingness of the human experience. Poetry is a riveting piece of music, and I think I explore that lyrically, there is potential. Dylan Thomas' famous line explains what this book is about, "rage, rage, against the dying of the light."

Acknowledgments

I would like to thank my two dear sons Possum, and Yuri for being a monumental inspiration to me. I would like to thank my partner for helping me come back to life and supporting me in everything that I do.

Thanks my loves, if it wasn't for you guys I would not have been able to finish this book.

Special Thanks
I would also like to thank the wonderful artist Freya (rurouni_drawings) you can find her on Instagram. She did an amazing job on my book cover.

DUST

I suppose we carry each

Other's emotions along

The perilous journey.

Carrying this heart

into the dust.

Seeing again each other

One day.

AUSTRALIAN HONEYSUCKLE

an Australian Honeysuckle
touches you and you
think of all the melodies
that have been lost
in arguments and how
frayed in bone you
feel, my love my honeysuckle
I do not fret, you whiten
my smile with a cosmic
unknown.

LEVITATE

Levitating on the silences
of mountainous
pictures of our
minds at rest,
levitating on
the lyric
of Old Beach
that lightning storm
I say to myself
I must be the air
I must be with you.

HEART

my heart is
a séance of death writhing in
the deepest catacombs of the
unknown, aghast,
& death purposes
love, yet I'm
not disappointed
I'm alive, dancing,
waltzing meandering
in a dreamless night like
Sappho is a shadow
of lilacs interceding
my life.

LITTLE SAPPHIRE

In bed I am drunk
on those little
sapphires that
belong to your thighs
drunk on what
could've been.

TIBET

Soft mist soft
dust of fragrant
delight we are
in Tibet watching
the snow fall
slowly
slowly you love
me again

DEBIT CARD

Eternity
Locks you
Up Stockholm
Syndrome
a relapse my
Leather jacket
Kills, and it kills
Me, smelling of
Dead burning
Smoke, puffing
on money, a lime
Drink, and I paid
For you to get lost
But I ran after our
Track sync in hail
We will never rail
The failed cost
For nothing more
Than a hidden
Debit card
That was everything
to me, I wanted
Love to outlast.

NOVEMBER THE 4TH

You whip your hair back and turn to me. Your eyes confiscate my attention from the noise of mediocre conversation. The oceanfront is where we are sitting unabashed on a beach hardwood bench. It is November the 4th. It is our first time in California. The ocean wind spray thwarts and hurries a salty dewdrop from the face of its waters. It is splendid to have an escape to have a moment in love without other people; this is what I consider being the new start of an entirely new life.

You talk about Italian coffee, and Woody Allen films effortlessly. You put your hand on my thighs and whisper how much you love this poem by Anne Sexton. You cannot remember the title. All you know is that it was like a confession of passion; the scent of a the human heart.

As we watch the sun fade from the marina and as the fisherman are bringing in their lines for the day you say with ease that this is where you want to be for the rest of your life vicariously in love with this moment of the efficacious passion of two lovers sold to these shorelines of everlasting light.

STARLIGHT

A woman is dancing, bathing in
Blue roses, she is whimsical,
Greater than any day, beauty
Coursing through her veins,
Her Saturn, velvet, crystal dress
Dipped in honey, a paradise carrying
You away, on sunrays she walks
Like moonlight, brave, kind
With a rosy flair,
Her heartstring dress
Is your safe haven of starlight
Her eyelashes give you insight
Her passion for you is a dance to stay
If you love better than yesterday,
A woman is dancing, she is saturating
All the night's skies, she wears her
Veil a garland of wildflowers waiting to
Kiss you into May, her
Fluid breath entraps you beyond delight
Beyond the pearls of oceans that
Are holier than light.

TASMAN PENINSULA

the cyclical apparitions
of unending, and
undying melancholy
a dream of velvet spikes
of images pasted in shadow
like intense gout,
we of vagabond
and scarlet
maelstroms think
of Demeter mad
of the unnecessary
catastrophe of existing
the nausea
is the echo
that is shrouding
in our wounds
we are a petal
tragically unknown
to the beauty
that everyone gets
but for us
we sink into a garland
on the tip of the Tasmanian
Peninsula

DON'T YOU REMEMBER?

I don't want you to feel alone. I don't want you to feel helpless. Don't you remember that kiss renewed your feelings for me?

Don't you remember how deep love can be? Don't you remember what it feels like to be alone, and don't you remember how it feels like to be at home with your arms wrapped around my skin, and the allurement of fate and how falling in love is not just a necessity, but it is the realisation that life isn't all that cruel?

Don't you remember what it feels like to be appreciated and listened to? Don't you remember our mornings curled up together, and how we read books and how we forgot to go on Facebook, and we didn't care if somebody left a message for us? The sweetness of love, and the simplicity of forgetting that the world didn't exist, busied us.

Don't you remember the music, the rumba we did, and those sudden bursts of energy that shaped our feelings? The silences aroused you in between looking at the roses coming to life, and those long hikes in the moonlight and how we shared headphones together, and we drank gin and tonic and watched the days pass by with ease.

Don't you remember what it feels like to wake up at noon and the sheets covered our naked bodies, and the chorus of our laughs echoed off the walls, and there was a holy ambiance to this craziness we called our love, and the novels that stacked up against our eyes, and the hungry cat needy, garrulous, and lovely. Don't you remember it? The last raindrop in July.

NOVEMBER

Grab the umbrella and give me a little kiss before you go. You were pensive and focused on the despair of this departure, and shallow was the sweet desperation Andre felt lost. Mary said she didn't want you to go. I don't know what it will be like without you! I can't even think. It is okay to feel this way, you know, but I must leave as sordid so that you will have me. I have to go, I have to find my own way in this world.

We will meet again; our lips will touch again. I know that may seem unwritable, but it is the way of the world. Don't feel uncomfortable, don't feel alone. If you remember, me you won't regress. Your time will be easier, and you will simply feel better. Can you please help me with my luggage? I can't carry it to the terminal by myself. I can't do this by myself, you know that.

Stop thinking, my love, and start remembering what love is all about; watching the rain pour down as she left the terminal gate, Andre felt that this departure was the beginning of the story.

DARK INSIDE OF ME

The dark is surmountable, the light unmissable. Wandering off the beaten path like a wilding searching for pelt in winter. The obscurity of existence. I preferred to be genuflected with the death of the moment. Amid the torment of being pierced by the moonlit craziness of being lost in the wild woods. Afar afoot the cold, and strange night. The destination is amiss.

The scenery is nebulous. I awakened to the sight of a glowing moon. It seemed blood-like, bold, and immaculately odd. It was here I found a tree of a weird sort. A silver maple with blue leaves. It spoke in a sorrowful tone, an elegy of a damp and wandering mind.

The silver blood-soaked maple spoke to me and said these words. I have seen and accessed your kind. I have seen wars; I have seen famines; I have seen kingdoms fall I have seen comets, and lilacs brought to life. And people carrying corn to undernourished children. I have viewed all the worst of your kind. One thing has occurred more often with absolute certainty. You are never happy to live in the moment.

You are never happy to just love a flower. You've to always carry it to the next. Moment you are never ever happy with just holding the petals.

No, you hold so much that the color goes and the petals fall. The future is uncertain, and yet I have been here for three thousand years and one thing has stood the test of time and that the moment a flower lives it lives for the moment for its dance is many and bountiful and ample. Yet beyond that moment, the flower ceases to be, it ceases to exist. So I say this to you, as I give you oxygen. Do not think of the oxygen that you will get in the next moment. Think of the oxygen you get now, and only now for you will truly breathe.

SIMPLE

It's simple
the way you feel
it's simply the way
you look into my soul
a rose springing to
life, smile
is the sound of
bluebirds sleeping
it's simple this wonderful
life the way you make
the day into the sunlight
the way your lips
confide in the simple
music of legs entwined
the simpleness of you.

REVIVAL

This is the revival.
Demons rise, they
Do, but the human
Heart survives despite
The entropy of live,
We move on relentlessly
we will never bow to the
never-ending dark.

CONVENANT

lay down the covenant
of thy soul, endow your
music within me
force thy parchment
of dark embers that
are the cherubim of
seraphs, guide the
wood winds and
force your erotic
tongue onto me.

DO NOT FORGET

do not forget
how rain-soaked
our toes were
and how we would
talk of love engrossed
in a wintery shell.

MY SOUL

My soul is a tweed jacket
sweet stitched
from the Tweed River in
Scotland a holy ghost
dancing on the
fumes of a rainy
fantastic
love.

PROMETHEUS RHAPSODY

I could not love the darkness.
In the darkness I see myself,
like a cannon that contains
one million weeping angels,
each tear of my solitude
is my rest upon this cruel world.
for my existence means nothing.
For what soul could bear the
weight of such a task without
hanging a noose around
his own throat only
the strong live a why.
I see nothingness as
a great virtue to live by.
For it is in the darkness, I see the
truth, it is a Colosseum of beauty.
My mind is like the
ruins of Athens, an ancient war
that ends daily, it is
my melancholy fate.
My eyes see the world as a
dark orb containing blood
suffering sweat and anguish.
veins speak words of
prophets and of tongues
for the liver and brain are
one cognitive frame,

anxiety is a divine virtue
the requiems that write our diaries
are cut legs and broken bones,
the tailbone of friends, and the gout
of our love is a putrid mess above,
each shackle is an injustice to mankind
war famine and crucifixion
a lover's discourse for the future
can be bleak, mutilate the truth, politics
is a battle between monkeys
while the poor try to burn down
the banks that gain their lively days and years,
we are fouled and
anchored, each fabric is of skin stabbing
the wounds that sing the
gesticulation of ashes fiery to the mouth of
Cherubim trees malt castles pillage unknown
gossamer cities, habiliment to the feast of
misery events outside the isle of fleeting
Violins, Hesper consummates the air like
nothing was even fair, the lust of fires lust
of hyacinthine roses, brimstone doors
 unrequited dreary sandstone skies

BEAUTY IS HERE

There is a beauty that
I will legislate on the
minds of men and
women. A truth
beyond depiction.
Forgiveness is the only
crucible that mankind
shall hear the earth of
night of a love so wise.
the wine of the blind.
see me in the lines
of the kind.

DOMINION

Where has the day gone but night?
Where has the heart gone but death?
Where has the sun been seen?
Conquer heathens, scattered blood
Upon the night, remembering such love.
Long have we been, dust to be left.
And such men deserve beauty
And such men deserve courage.
Risen is he who doesn't mangle,
Risen is the one who doesn't strangle.
Yield unto the deserved sun
Yield unto the deserved gun.
Where has the gone
all these verses continue to murk
Into the wood, from the last kiss to the sun?
Beneath me, the dominion of nothingness
Beneath us, beneath the trails ablaze
Somebody will be brave and see the night.
The night has come—we are alive in such light.
Wanders into the Lord of might.

JOY OF SPARROWS

The joy of sparrows
and the spring of youth.
the heavens behave as
we yearn for them too
the maelstroms,
the Sufi mystics the
Fibonacci cactuses.
Love spiraling towards
the verses in your
sins, wherever the
The truth is there is a mockery.
we are in the streets
of Amsterdam, you cannot
be stifled until you have seen
the face of naked love.
Vases of ecstasy,
tonics of serenity
bliss; every day.

BEHEMOTH

Behemoth could
never compromise zenith,
nor could the shadows accrue,
or dispense the deep,
and habitual unease
of Ulysses,
the occultism of
of pleasantries
forgive my larks for
their incandescence.
Are the echelons of
our hymns the
ad nauseam of an
unworthy heart?
The heart is owned
and rented out by the
shadows, the light
ought to give us clarity
and it will.

SODDEN

Nature itself is undulating
inside of you. Nature is
a libidinous maniac, a corset
of magma, nature, protruding
valleys, anointing Ophelia with
sadness, upon chastising the ruin
of our cloudy emerald eyes,
we do not want to be understood,
and will do everything vocally
possible to be misunderstood,
wordless winds, untouched
hymns, sodden limbs
glory a downpour
sanctified
on your smooth
legs.

MYTHOLOGISING

We were mythologizing the
sunlight, pretending we
were it, we are not the coldness
of the universe. Our rib cages
hold the/crimson rainbows
we are personifying the
the bluest moon dipping our
hands in hemlock
we carried/songs
into our memories.
brutal love, honesty
saccharine/purity
tenebrous/galaxy
stop and see\our
only kiss/ an agape
melody

WHERE DOESN'T THE ROAD GO?

Oh, the lonely veins of our melody
relinquishing the slush of reason
in some dream somewhere.
in the nowhere song where I sleep
where love is the being of treason,
rapturous dexterity of the wounded
you cannot surprise me.
The critics desire, and yearn for acceptance
the pariahs, the gargoyled monochrome sky
blood oozing and flowing through the rice
fields dancing like honey, the metaphors
come, apocalyptic musings stapled to the
minds of men, shrapnel valleys gorged
with the silence of un-awakened
grace, nobody knows, the dark cruel
moss on the cadavers, war is the yoke
of humanity.

VIOLATING VIOLET

rosy violent bloodstain
a vase of sunlight corroding
your mindless beauty
therein the shadows be me,
drink my hemlock—see me
emerald purple rain,
purified moon forgetfulness,

a wasteland of your misery
we see the kinked stars,
blond oceans, sylphlike thighs
Are you the princess of choice?
the rues, and dandelions follow your
victory now, hush the darkness
a farrowing life, harrowing light
gallows contrite, love is right

MOONLIGHT DEATH

there is nothing
more than the moonlight
sweeping away our prejudices
into the morning for us to peel
off our egos. to be submissive
to grace is to respond to fear
with a playful heart.
there is languidness
to fear and there is love
wrapped in a storm that
is what fear is; a storm yet
to be driven through sails
ahead, take your wildflowers
to the poor and become free
with them. I pray for them
my prayer is of the moonlight,
my prayer commands death
and I urge my foes to pick
wildflowers for the poor,
for only then will they
be free

BROWN HAIR

Your brown
hair is versed
in gale force
winds, your
neck honeyed
in charlotte
rivers, touch
prurient moonlight
encased in your
lingerie,
drowning in Ophelia
you see the sunset
weaving you into an
undulating
sorrow

RESURGENCE

You make the light
less boring than
all the preachers do.
you have a prerogative
that soothes thunder
into laughter, joy becomes
complexity and the rain
becomes flesh, whenever regret
frequents me; your starry
nature commences its
own agenda in the boardroom
of my heart where all my meeting
minutes are darkness, your sweet
attitude makes me plummet
into a sweet bitter
resurgence.

SCENT OF YOU

The deep shadow inverted
on my mind, glorious sublime
the sweat, and allure of passing,
and dying in the ponds of light
and I suffocate in your kind moonlight,
grand, and evolving into endless arms
confiscating the voice of Gaia's life,
I see / and am aroused by the
the emptiness of a river bed gorged
in neglect, see the bluebird
it will be your friend, the only truth
that exhausts you in nature's scent.

PESSOA

I still
have Fernando
Pessoa inside me
orchestrating my
existential whims
of unshakeable
hymns and
here I go
where the sea
is dimmer than snow
dimmer than all my
potential woes
a shimmering across
a vastness of emotion
that couldn't destroy
our pure joy.

BACKWOODS

The backwoods
has your saliva entrenched
in its beating melody
like a sun of unknown
silence you shine through
foggy nights of regret
of daisies alive
in the afterglow
in the afterglow
a wolf of snow
heaven of
tumultuous flow.

APRIL MY PARIS

Wherever jazz
welcomes
the downtrodden
you will
find an Eden
more peculiar
and alive as
the sun dancing
silhouetted in the
psalm of
Charlie Parker's
April In Paris.

ODE TO MISERABLE ME

I'm eluded by the fate of my old lines, the old lines of a dirty writer, the old lines of a dirty miserable me an ode to myself. I'm lifelessly in love with the frustration I receive from a soggy kiss. Whenever a woman doesn't want me I open up this ode to miserable me, and I let the trivialities rot my consciousness. The glories of love are far too shadowy to share with one poem. There's no phrase in heaven or earth that could relinquish my doubtlessly unknown brain to give up my love for writing the stanza in the most sadistic, and doleful way possible.

I sit on a thornless throne of golden ivy remembering that the opera song of my thoughts is to be shared with one maiden of who is going to owned by hands, and my silver jaded smile. It's kind of like a prison of ivy. I guess as I try, and repeat this again the throne I sit on also is an uterus of a ascetic pillar bespangled with daisies, and daphnes are going to be the varnish to the floor of my story. And I own all the words of fiery breasts, my words shaped these breasts of the most aesthetic women in existence my stories created godless creatures. My stories created beauty so unfathomable that my stories bring forth creamy mango froth from the chambers of your heart.

The nothingness sitting outside is incomparable with anything I've touched. I'm lonely, I'm lonesome, and attracted to the shades of this rigid nothingness. I wrote a decadent ode to miserable me in the half-moon of the leafless sunset, as the melancholic leaves fell, I fell too with the blooming shades of the abysses that gave birth to more odes for my agony.

I know the source of my endless pain it lies within the inebriated stars I swallowed long ago. For what's endless does have an end that's less than our heart's expectation of a strong passionate, heartfelt ode to me. The ode to miserable me was a memory; a memory of unjust light, and an unjust colouring of the light, for it is in the light that you truly find me.

For the stars are drunk from our cosmic and subtle presence. Neither the vitality of the drunken stars could fill the nothingness in every abyss of every human being born to die in the graceless blindfolds that cover our combusted eyes. Nothingness can saturate our souls with banal memoirs of unforgotten trails that we once walked, my dear revengeful liar.

ON THE WAY TO FORBES

The world was a big place for our family's silver Toyota Tarago. We would go to Forbes on weekends to get away from city life. Traveling to Forbes was always an adventure.

Most of the time, I was glued to my phone, playing Pokemon Gold on the way. But my mum would say, " Jeremy, turn that off and look out the window. Look at the world. Don't get sucked into mindless activities. Let your mind wander to the green pastures. "
The further I looked through the windows on the way to Forbes, the more I felt like I was living in a dream. The greener pastures fade through the incorruptible sunlight. Ewes eating vast amounts of hay, horses galloping forevermore. There was a kind of music to the way the cattle prodded along.

I saw beauty and fields, yellow fields, canola flowers, and one of the most important aspects of our trips was trying to figure out what animal was what. It was a game we used to play as a family to pass the time since the trip was nearly an hour and a half. It was good to sit back and relax, turning on the old Beach Boys cassette track. We would stop at Eugowra to see Poppa. Poppa was very interesting, and he was a good gardener. He had some apple trees and a vast amount of vegetables.

I used to love running around and being pushed in the wheelbarrow. There was a really nice place with prehistoric rocks that were piled on top of each other. I used to let my imagination run wild, and I saw these little caves as openings into another universe.

I was a really good storyteller, and I would soak in the surroundings. I knew there was a story behind every tree, and behind every ant nest, there was a story. All I had to do was repeat it to myself.

AT ULURU

At Yulara, we camped in complete darkness under the starlit sky. You desired my arms, and it felt natural. Our legs were entwined like Babylonian vines. It was music for you to hold. It was a holy experience to be with you.

I could not remember the world when I was with you. You were the dream time. You were that silence I always yearned for. I could see your warmth in the scintillating moonlight.

You made Uluru complete. You journaled your heart on my sinew. And your flesh becomes a part of me. It might sound cliche to say it was like holding the sun, but I don't care you made me feel good and I know life is cruel, and we should try to be happy.

You made reading love stories so pure, and you brought all the mountains of the world with you. And I felt the sorrow, and love of the great mist that flowed and waltzed from your body onto my lips. My body shivered in truth and I felt the sleep I had always wanted to die in with you with your lips covering my bruises. I soul you, and I venerate your smile, and I seek to know you more. Under these stars at Uluru, all truth beauty smothered by you.

THE FISHERMAN FROM BURNIE

I have been transported to the ward after waiting in the emergency room for eight hours because of a flare-up of my inflammatory bowel disease. For the first time, I got a ward bed instead of the chaotic one in an emergency this time. I get some comfort. As I am transported from the lower floor of the hospital to the upper floor, I am calm. I have done this before. I have no anxiety or stress, and I feel perfectly at peace with myself.

I hear the fading shrieks of newborn babies and an old woman crying out in anguish. I am still okay and not affected. As an orderly transports me in a wheelchair, I am solemn. As we get to the room, he helps me onto the bed. I lie down and cover myself in the hospital blanket. There is another person in the room, grumpy, but down to earth. He has a long beard and looks like Alan Moore. He has tubes going in and out of his body, feeding him morphine intravenously.

He has a hard heart like Huon pine and does not get swayed by all the theatrics of being in hospital. He says, ''Hey Jeremy, it is going to be an okay ride." I say well, I hope it gets better for you. He tells me he has three weeks to live. Jesus, take it one day at a time, buddy.

What do you do for a living I ask him calmly, "I'm a fisherman from Burnie." You have a beard like Alan Moore, I remark again, how are you so euphoric about your death? I have lived enough. We all have to die. At some point, acceptance is the alleviation of that philosophical problem. I overheard you calling your family and loved ones earlier. I didn't hear you cry once. You are so at peace with it all. Well, I am not at peace with it, really. I mean, we all want to live forever, right? It is not set in stone how long we are here for.

All you can do is take each day as it comes. I mean, what is the point of creating commotion when there is no need to? As my father once said to me, a fisherman is a man who has been in patience with death since he started throwing the line in the water. There ain't no cure for death, but if we take each minute as a blessing, the trawl will feel much longer.

I remember sitting at the edge of the water many times, and not catching anything. Half the point is in the wait, the other half is the catch, and if you catch anything, you are lucky. Take your life as it comes, be in communion with nature, respect the everlasting flow of time. These idealisms might seem weird and downright illogical, but self-acceptance is all about accepting the things you can't change. You should get some rest; sometimes the best rest you'll ever get in a ward.

NAUSEA

I heard gunshots being fired from two blocks down. The sun faded above the skyline, and at a distance, I saw the crisp king tide rolling in sweetly. I had a vintage blue silk tie on with a green tweed coat. I wasn't sure what tomorrow would bring. Nobody did. I could only estimate that there would be a fair few misgivings and a fair few complaints.

I had worked all day in the office trying to arrange appointments with clients and faxed many important letters to the head of staff. There was a slow death in doing things like this, and all I could ask for was a Cuban cigar and genuinely nice whiskey. I would go to the local bar to try to pick up a lady for a good time. Every time I would try to pick up someone, I'd get nausea, the kind Sartre talked about in his book Nausea.

I liked being alone. I revelled in the reverie of being on my own watching the sunset and the moonlight dragging the wind down the street in the darkness like a lonesome wayward siren. I didn't lack confidence or hope, I just lacked meaning. I read plenty of books on that subject matter, but nothing filled me. Nothing was gained, not even from stapling my hand to a desk chair. The only beauty I got was fantasy; I'd look at a young blonde broad, and the thought of doing something frisky was terribly pleasing. I didn't want to go further. There is a maxim to be found in watching the sunset and doing nothing. Maybe you should try it.

RAINED

You idyllically saw the hollowness of existence as a dance, and you danced to jazz with purity and gamble. You of holy origin, piercing and evocative, a book collector and novel thinker, take the rain by its balls. You make the storm yours.

I remember when you pulled out a gun on that library clerk and stole that prized Faulkner book for me. We ran and caught a train like Kerouac.

We'd make love in cotton fields, and see the corn come to life at harvest. You'd melt into shadow at night and slip the moonlight into your eye sockets because you coursed like flowing blood.

You saw beauty when the road ended, and you drank as Jesus did at his last supper. You had verbosity like a lion and the legs of an Aphrodite. You saw the road and its undying possibilities of finding the truth.

BRIGHT DARK

Unencumbered in my tomb of relentless indifference. I was free of the aloofness that came with entering into the social domain of human interactions. My heart was growing weary, numb, and unafraid. I sought to close my eyes to the negligence of human society.

The solemn wind blew against my neck as I was staring into the deep cataclysm of the sweet buried summer that was evaporative and beautiful. Though I was awake, I was dead in silence, and the swiftness of melancholy bludgeoned me. I was in Kafka's trial, burdened by the angst and harrowing sorrow of existence.

The disquieted moonlight solidified my marrow as I felt the pulse of a disheartened rhapsody. The melody of destruction, the pettiness of deep despair, rigid and sparse in complexity, I assumed death ought to happen to me.

The echoes of grief I could hear from the great mess of algae on the bayou. So beautiful was the transparent night glow, the sweeping, torrential darkness that beat my skin fervently and passionately.

There is a beauty to this nightmare, this brusque language of death, this semantic deviation, this collapsing shadow that I am a vessel of. I felt the consequences of my mistakes in my prison of a mire, where the black swan is a flame of my own deathless love.

THE RIVER

I fucking mean it, Ben, hand me the cigarettes now. I don't care. I genuinely care about Ben. I don't care if you smoke them; I care that you're lonely and unhappy. I care that all you can see at every turn is a thick fog. We're out for a walk in the woods in Maine. I couldn't remember precisely where we were, but all I could think about was the sharp cold consuming our flesh.

"Hurry up," I said to Ben, "we don't have all day. We have to get going in the morning before the sun hits the trees. It was nearly midnight, and we were bewildered, like the mania of King Macbeth. I didn't know what to do. Ben was always a reclusive young chap, devoid of meaning. I put out his cigarette, and he got really mad. Don't you fucking do that again? Do I want to feel dead? I want to feel alone. Well, you aren't fucking alone. I am here with you. Stop your swearing, I said. Well, you just swore at me, hypocrite. I had a bottle of old tequila in my backpack, and the night kept on following us like a spectre on cocaine.

I was the only person Ben could talk to, and he felt okay with me. I felt okay with him too. We loved walking in the woods. We would go for a few days every month to escape city life. There was something pure in the woods, and I can't put my finger on it, but it was a feeling that was strong. It felt like the world would fade away.

I didn't care about tomorrow, and neither did Ben. We loved arguing about politics and who was in power. I would always end up making sure that Ben won, so he felt he had gained some ground. We pitched our tents near the river, and the sweet shadow danced off the hoods of our tents.

The next morning, we ate some peanut butter on rye bread, accompanied by some bacon. Ben stomped on the ground. Maybe Cormac McCarthy was right. Maybe there is no God, and we are his prophets. First things first, nobody has proved the existence of God, and secondly, the beauty of life is that the answer is individualistic. The only answer you can have is the answer you fight for.

Ben stomped again and said, "I want to go home. I said, "No, we ain't going home. We came out here to find ourselves. I am going to stay with you until you stop smoking. I don't care if we stay in the rain, or if we are so cold that it stamps out the senses of reality, you are going to go on, and you are going to defeat this. We went on foot, and the unfolding river stretched out as far as the rain faded, and we had each other and the endless pathways to the light.

SOLITUDE

It was idealism that made tomorrow a possible thought. As perplexing as that is, the moment I met you in that restaurant four years ago was the day I started to take the idea of Zen seriously. I mean, who knew that one casual conversation would create a conversation that would last longer than expected? I mean, we are so busy trying to find our way in this world that we never take the time to appreciate those quiet moments drinking coffee and speaking about things that obviously entangle our eyes in a void of subjectivity.

There was no other basis for it. I was drawn to what I wanted to discover. I was drawn to what love could do for me. Is that not the truth? Is that what Hamlet postulated? That we are stars trying to find our sense of brevity, our sense of clarity? The only things that were logical to me were those passing moments seeing the mountain mist swallow the mountain whole, and how we would venture into far off desolate places that made us uncomfortable, and time went fast. It felt really good in your hands, warm and true.

The moment we try to think about tomorrow, we are already signing our names on the casket of life. There is more beauty in the beaten-up path, and I have no other inkling than this that love is found in cafes, jazz, and mountain walks alone, or with someone who shares the spirit of solitude.

SILENCE WITHIN SILENCE

I wanted nothingness
and it desired my heart
to take all my memories
and turn them into ash,
this world has always
been too much for
my heart to swallow,
it's a poison that
melts
the rose
inside
my chest,
people are too much for
me, I feel awkward around
them as if I was a ghost
invisible to their communication
I've always had problems
with socialising.
people cannot see under
lies, I don't feel alright
I'm the nightingale
with ongoing suffering
and grief,
my guts
spell out
misery and
desolation a musical

to everyone else
but me
hands clutched my head,
it feels like my skull
is about to explode
the words write
death when I
type it makes
me feel better.

UNDERSIDE

The underside of
the heart is complex,
rhythmic fire soothing,
kisses of night, lissome
voluptuous days
always surprise.
in death there is
sex, in light there
is something kind.
the moonlit wreck
of who we are is
in the songs of
Johnny Cash.
the signature
of love is always
a try, a rhyme of
signs in a violin
of air, you
hear the cheek
of might

MIND

Sometimes
 I feel like that
I write too many poems
sometimes my
 mind tells me stop,
but then my heart reminds
me that this is for my soul
that by writing poetry
 I'm doing my duty
 for nature itself.

AUSTRALIAN SUMMER

I can smell the ode
of an Australian summer,
dry like honey-baked rye bread.
shortness of green in
the ferns, bushfires galore.
barbecue spirited life,
I can smell the burning off
leaves. Nobody wants a bonfire.
only the beaches belong to us in the
Summer, I can smell the Australian
summer, I can smell more brutal
then the sweet taste of bacon
and cheddar cheese, I can smell
the Australian summer working
In the sun. This Australian summer
is a demon unto itself,
all you want is a bit of shade
and rum ice and a book
To pass the time. My hot steel-cap
boots are under the rivers of
a desert sea of that Australian summer

MOONBEAMS

the eclectic moonbeams
on your blue hair
causes me to question
my own existence.
such beauty shouldn't
exist in a universe
of complete bedlam.
I am air-kissed to death
just by seeing
you wake up,
how can beauty exist
in a universe like this?

RIBS

your ribs
withstands all I know
even Siberian snow even
what I can't sow
be my lady in the storm
give the night sky form
shoulder the rain kiss
me in Kuwait
where the lavenders
wait like that oak tree
near the ocean bend
where our story
is palming our faithless
light, and when you live?
you'll be alright
keep me near
you needn't fear
when you got that kiss
stored in your bones
in your bones near
the ocean road

CURSED

It was easy to feel like the world didn't belong to you. I slipped into the ease of my shadow. The world was fictional and excessive in structure. The smell of lavender was my home; it was better to be persuaded by the sorrow of existence to lie alone in undulating moonlight. There was a revelation in how a deer's carcass faded and deteriorated, and how the leaves were soft and mushy before winter.

And I succumbed to fear and its beautiful poison. Nothing seemed to matter, only the cat's purr and the slow, riveting motion of seeing the sun go down. If you saw the world as it really was, if you saw it created and if you saw the slow death of time, you'd want to never rise again. You wouldn't want to see butterflies. You'd see the moroseness take you away. You'd see it flow lovingly. As the dark bone of existence was florid and deathless, you will awaken again to the same day and the same sun dying.

BODY

A misty
cave ruby like
with loveliness
overflowing and
and an overgrowth
of wild white roses
scintillation in melody
entrenching our walks
on the shore with a smoothness
like a lost river finding its
way through the world
you awaken in me a
terrible longing
for a tide that never
glows and a moonlight
that overthrows our
purgatory

DYLAN THOMAS IN ME

The freedom of possibility is one of the divine pleasures of agnosticism. Because I don't know why or how I exist, I can't call myself an atheist. Everything I know about life is melodic, chaotic, and poetic. I cannot say with certainty that my existence or life in general has a purpose. I cannot be certain that there will be a tomorrow, just as I cannot be certain that today will end.

All I know is that time is what we have, and the only utility in this thing called life is to play along with the song. As far as philosophy is concerned, this is all I know, and perhaps I might be wrong, but at least I had a crack at this exceptionally impossible and seismically tough question: whether there is a point to existence. Perhaps you might have the answer that I am looking for, as Dylan Thomas said, "I hold a beast, an angel, and a madman in me."

PORCELAIN RIVER

she sold me a river
of porcelain letters
and I drowned in
daybreak, only to find
her dress waiting for
me in the sunlight, her
the spirit is gone without a clue,
hidden in the fluorescent hues
in the glory of a ruined rue

HONEYSUCKLE

How peaceful love can
be, how joyous and grateful
you can be when you are not
looking to be the victim
hero, love is the hero if you
are trying to be the victim.
you are the darkness and
the darkness has you.
how fleeting men are
when they are not the
chapters of their own lives
how cruel, how hereditary
is the sinfulness in their
hands, love is the hero.
you must be it, see it,
breathe it, and plant
the honeysuckles
for all.

IMMANENT

immanency in a beguiled kiss,
buried in seas of withered
moonlight there is a winter
fox, he looks at your gown.
The mystery gives you a crown.
I here that beauty cannot be
anticipated, nor cannot it be
displayed without your authority
in the wondering bliss of your
neck

COLONISATION

There was a shimmering wombat
in the darkness near the western
Billabong, and a fascinating silence.
Kangaroos of the Lachlan lingering
at the edge of the coolness. there
are yellow bellies flowing in the
the grace of the Lachlan,
the darling robins
of the morning sing an unsung leaf
of summer, king brown snakes, smoke at
Ophir near Orange, dry riverbeds.
gold is hidden under loose ground
around the necked shaped coolabahs
there was an unconventional
rhythm to the disturbed dwellings
of the Wiradjuri people, their ghosts
in the fallen red gums from
the colonisation long ago.

MYRRH MOONLIGHT

Her eyes are consumable.
netted in the cheeks of
heaven, a myriad of myrrh
moonlight, and
her eyelids sing
devilishly, songs
of tomorrow
songs of sorrow
songs of tomorrow
songs, of straw skies
emerald water.
if only you could
forget the dark.
oh, my juniper
oh, my heaven
oh, my earth
oh, my breath
oh, my death.

INFINITIES

Infinities beyond,
in the graveyard of
perpendicular
delirium trees.
wherein doubt, jealousy
die a dismal fate.
all bodies rise
in the guilt of
winking pottery.

clay is the destiny of all men.
Love is the destiny of all clipped skies.
to be unloved is to be scrapped
from the heavens of uncapped
mercy.

all the elements of unrequited
stables of coffins are, but a
lapse in a timeless adventure
to the ingredient of your
fingers.

SUSPICIOUS

I've lied for a century.
I've had a face full rain
because I've wondered what
it'd be like to know you.
I've forgotten the home I used
to love, I have forgotten sophisticated
words, I've forgotten the
the way you used to love me.
I have a face full of tears in the
rain. I know you've suspicious
smile unrelenting, and sound
I've tackled all the griefs of your
past and I just want to slam them
down with the breath I've now.

UNHOLY

I feel your breath knotted around my
chest. your breath turns my fear into an
erotic symphony of impulsive sin
this sin, this rejection of God
you terrify me amazingly
with your forbidden sensual deathbed.
I cherish this voodoo of
unholy graces.

DON'T WRITE HURTFUL LOVE
SONGS

All the love songs
don't have to be the same,
they could be more than insane,
they could be so fucking loud
filled with ego, and the profound. how
can one ever write a love
song if

you've never learned how to be
crazy, wearing a straitjacket is okay,
don't try to be normal
you'll only be cheating yourself

don't write me, hurtful love
songs, don't write me hurtful
love songs, don't write me
hurtful love songs,

don't write
love songs, only write them
if you're insane, write about sin
write about lyrical decay.
don't write me, hurtful love
songs unless you're insane,
okay?

don't write love songs
unless you've been wrong
baby, don't write me a
love song unless you can
be wonderful and strong

MEANING OF FIRE

It's courageous to be deceived
by love, to be infatuated with
fear and doubt, to find the labyrinth
to the meaning of fire
is the reason one has to find,
the meaning of fire is endorsed
by the privilege of knowing hell,
but the privilege of knowing
love far outweighs the persistent
challenges one finds in death,
to enter love without
regret, to enter love without
neglect, to enter love without
intellect is the answer to being,
we are too late to live in reality
because we're too
busy living in the imagination of love.
one must be a voiceless hummingbird, a
skylark of the tenebrous to find the
meaning of our fire, the hearthside is our
prerogative , the hearthside is love.

DAVID BOWIE WITH US

We walked through
fields of lavender together.
our arms held the spirit
of David Bowie's music together.
because our joyfulness was
David's last mellifluous breath,
David be with us in the
hostile wind, sing some Ziggy
into us make us your labyrinth of
creative godliness.

HUMMINGBIRD

We were two zealous hearts
made of feathers. alone, unafraid
of what's in our fires of lonesomeness
my beloved knew how to
dance out of the phosphorescent decay
of the day, we were featherless unafraid
we were okay,
we were okay,
we were two hummingbirds
seeking glory,

hearts featherless, we were okay
because my beloved, I'll never be
okay without you being featherless.
because when I die my feathers live
on in the stardust of your crimson
peacock feathers.

LEVIATHAN

Leviathan of the ruby amber
abyss covered in labyrinths of
the past. a tenebrous
sorrow of lucifer,
the incarnate isn't
sparse, multitudes
of darkness
wrapped in
the spine of
Medusa.
the careless dwarf stars
pulsate the pebbles of the
red sea, lonely in the
end, only this
negligent firmament
illuminates the
befallen nonchalant
Zeus.

SPANISH RUM

I could smell the fresh blue ink lingering in the wastebasket. I could smell centuries of sadness, lovebirds dying cyclones arriving. I didn't pay much attention to Jill. She was all-loving, but she was also bellicose. There was a sense of something missing an entire lifetime that faded before my eyes. Our pictures were wasted, our old wedding gifts, and steel butcher knives were thrown away.

What did I miss? Was I there enough for her? Didn't I love her enough? Did I not take her to Madrid last summer? We were so content beyond imagination, our stomachs filled with love and the greatest of Spanish rum.

Something has cracked inside of us. We have grown apart. I didn't pay attention to her. I mean, I filled this wastebasket with torn love letters, seared in tears and red wine. Maybe it was a sign I needed to move on. Perhaps I needed to write my love letters to her. We did leave some things unfinished. Something was amiss, but how could I salvage something from nothing? We broke up a week ago, and the wastebasket was not empty.

The ink was strong and affectionate; it was warm and cold; it lingered on. If I linger with it, then I will become the letter in the wastebasket. I will not move on. I will write my letter and I will take it to her, and I will kiss it and I will give her my whole body. I will give her my entire attention. My attention shall no longer be in the wastebasket. I will pay attention to the things that matter, and that's her smile.

SWIMMING

Singing and swimming
between two black melodies
sun drawn in disbelief
a solemn crossing
a dividing range
in your skin a
dagger of antipathy

CYPRESS

We watched the blue shining
diaphanous divinity of the Cypress
rivers lyrically dance in tune
with our consciousnesses and
rebirth was upon us like a
vesper of a forgotten
effigy that shrunk
in a Mediterranean shadow
drunk on this event this tempestuous
reverie waiting for a speck of snow
a Raindrop but nothing was suspended
from the heavens for you
the grace you were desirous of
evaporated without a trace
not even a grain of dark love
would awaken to our lost
thoughts that faded
with those rivulets today

ALASKA

The Alaskan frost is deeper
but not wider than your eyes
and I think of vultures circling our
melody, fresh is this storm of love
storm of arms touching the origin
of grace, a season to regret
a season to find and accumulate
beauty in our veins
beauty in our veins like
a dead magnolia imprisoned in your
ears all you want to know is beauty
you don't want to fall into this lake
this gigantic snake my beautiful
cannot be slain you are like
Nabokov on fire
a dark daffodil left on the doorstep
left in the cold but time cannot fold
that feeling of being lost in
Prague's wild paths are a beauty
we know better than the
descent of the dark

JARRAH

Whispers of fallen
Jarrah trees swallowed
up by the big dry
dust storms wayward
in Coober Pedy
light drowning
footprints
Eastern grey kangaroos
drifting away into
spacious silence
the land is awake
it moves the shadows
of my ancestors around
forevermore like
a song of honey ants
that is raw.

CENTRAL PARK

As I stared at the drooping dark silhouette of rain that was hazy and sprawling like an eternal ghost storm that enclosed all the city, I saw two men outside of the cafe smashing in a car with baseballs, yelling something about COVID-19. I could've called for the police, but I watched as a spectator and it was easier to do nothing. It was easier to see the scene and how the object of pursuit was eviscerated.

I could've had some moral backbone, I could've stopped them, I could've fought for justice! But I didn't. I ordered my coffee and walked out of the cafe. I gave the barista four dollars, and I thanked him.

I put on my tweed coat and walked out onto the busy Brooklyn pathway. The noise of reality was unsettled, but I was okay. Nothing was happening, and I was pretty sure that nothing was going to happen tomorrow either. I was bored with reality.

I loved being alone. It was like a religion for me; I loved being inside a church that was unpopulated. I like walking alone in the rain with a bagel in one hand and a cappuccino in the other.

I didn't want to go home just yet; I walked to Central Park, and there was so much noise that I had to find a tree somewhere near a little stream. I sat down on the ground and gazed at the stretching shadow rain that enclosed the city as far as the eye could see. It was comforting to know that the city was gorged in mist. It was beautiful to see reality smothered.

STARWARD

"Starward is where I want to be," she said coldly, aloofly, shrivelled up! "I am drawn to the stars and the paths they take." I know there is a certain acuity required to comprehend the freshness of chaos and the divergence that comes with it, as well as the misery that results from experiencing it. I was always thinking about the marriage of being the anticipative feeling, the wondering of love.

And I have arrived at such a state of catharsis that I see the overwhelming force of love that comes about when one is accepting the chaos as a natural fabric of existence. When I see the stars. Our kisses are a living album of truth, she said in her poignant musing that by arriving at the understanding that love is always starward.

At the end of this song, she thought of all the things that were going to keep her alive, and one recurring sound was the heartbeat and the naturality of togetherness.

TWO HANDS

Two hands on your shoulders
forty breaths lost in Boulder
Your blue suede high boots
the taste of New York rain
that abandoned elegy
you sound like spiralling waves
in a Turin lake
my eyes drunk
in the clouds that make my
soul heavy your smile
your legs pressed against my
chest the night feels longer
than life but you walk like an
acoustic bluebird
my sweet lonely
fog I am shipwrecked
and all I got are these
lines the ones I've found
in the veil of your shadows
my green rose
forevermore an echo
this winter burns my
arms I got your dreams
held in my arms
I am waiting for you
call me sometime my
only tear

FADING ROSE

How did you come to love me? She expressed her excitement. Rose was my lover in the hospital, battling leukemia. Well, I'm sure you didn't fall in love with me until we met at that cafe. You were wearing white rose garlands in your hair.

But I swear, from that moment, all I wanted was to take your body and drive all the way from Albuquerque to that forest in Denver. But I know it was not love at first sight for you.
You took your time. I mean, love isn't consistent or all-powerful. It often works like necromancy. But I know you love to hit the road with everything left behind.

Our Cadillac The sun sets on your red-tinged hair, your arms out the windows watching the trees disappear. I can't lie any longer. The first time I really laid eyes on you wasn't when we bumped into each other at that cafe in Sydney. It was at that time at the LA library that I laid eyes on you. I knew you so well, and I could see you reading Faulkner intensely. You certainly fell in love when we fed those pigeons in Brooklyn. I know you didn't want to admit it. But I know your soul perfectly now, better than my own, I think. Rose took another aspirin and held my arm strongly. Please tell me more about the hearse and the road.

"Well okay, I sighed for a moment, as troubled as my memory was, because grief can inflict a great deal of misery on the human heart. I continued with my yarn, well you remember the time we stole that bike in Amsterdam?" And we were high. Hugh, don't change the subject. Tell me when your heart started beating for me.

Well, I actually saw you at that Bob Dylan concert. You were buying a beer from the bar-stand. You were so magical. I thought I was being delusional. You had a pink and blue dress on with your hair tied back, and you had raw, crushingly red cheeks, lips wrought by Aphrodite herself. I knew from that moment that I would meet you again and again until we died together, but I wasn't hoping that you would get sick. But I knew I had to have you, and I didn't care about the odds. I knew life was miserable. I mean, that is a standard truth of existence.

You accentuated a presence that needed to be preserved, loved, and consumed like bluebirds dancing in mountainous fog. I was going to ask you out as I was still groggy. But I needed to do it more formally. I didn't want to come off as a creep. So I purposely bumped into you at that cafe. I needed to make fate happen. Screw the universe. Screw organised religion. I was going to organise the universe for once, and a world without you in it is not a world worth living in.

Rose took more water and sobbed more. Well, I am glad that you did that. Otherwise, who else would have listened to my nonstop stories about how aliens exist? I chuckled a bit, and took Rose's hand more. I knew that any moment could be her last, and we continued talking.

CANCER NOTE

She yanked on my arm, tears streaming down her cheeks. She was perplexed and troubled as to why she had died so young. Don't be concerned, my love. I'm here to keep you safe in this vast unknown, and I know the seas are rough. I don't want to die alone. I don't want to see the sun without your honesty and your legs wrapped around mine. She cried. More grief engulfed her skin. She was agitated and troubled by the prospect of her death. Her brow furrowed in the depths of the abyss, tears streaming down her cheeks.

Death is not easy and it is harder than life. From the moment we are born, we start dying. We live in order to die. But we do not die in order to live. My love, surely you know this, but you are not alone in this.

My kisses will help you sleep. My heartstrings are anxious about this too. My love, I will hold your body, and the deep cold you think you are entering will be warmer for a part of you won't die. It will live on in my memory of your love, and perhaps centuries from now, our kisses will be in paintings and in poems dedicated to the idea of not dying truly alone.

STAND

Standing in a folkish stream
fists clenched, an unforgettable
silver silhouette lifting our dreams
curing our trembling veins
mashed with the deification of
stray tabby cats in Toyko your love
reaches far beyond the north-western
clouds in Notre Dame everybody is crazy
everybody let's us down, but love is the
feverish tune we can relocate with.

TEQUILA IN TOKYO

The smell of your lavender skin
You are sitting there cross legged
Those Tokyo legs vibrant
Your hair curled with Jennifer Aniston's
Spectre of lustfulness, your sylphlike
Legs, I gnaw on them in my mind
I have already orgasmed in my mind
You are reading Murakami's Norwegian
Wood, you have the sinful vibrancy to your
Body, your eyelashes like a swift dark
Void filled with primroses and lilacs
I think that I want to buy you tequila.

IN BOGOTA

Lucid is the moment
Two angels in bed with me
In a Bogota motel, ravishing
Me exploring me, I am tied
Up their eyelashes and mascara
Penetrating my skin their nimble
Tongues caressing every square inch
Of my cock. I feel their asses one
Sits on my face, the kindling is beginning
I draw my last breath as the other mounts
My hard cock, the smell of apple cider
Is all over her breasts I am drunk I must
Be hallucinating.

HAVANA

As you read this; touch yourself
Touch your skin think of Havana
Think of the gorgeous bums lining
The beaches and the cigars that will
Be smoked during sex think of the
Wind, and the perfection of those
legs wrapped around your body
Think of the secret languages
Spoken during sex those orgasms
That speaks of luxuriation think
Of souls crushed in red wine
Bodies intertwining in the moonlight
Think of your own skin think of
Your own flesh wrapped around
The brutality of their beauty Latino
Maids and Latino milfs commuting
Into your soul, and touch yourself.

MEMPHIS

The river lights in Memphis
your boots redder than my veins
your smile quiet enough ataraxy
brought on by the closeness of
your delight pressed into my skin
Memphis is here in our minds for awhile

an ode to the corset you wore last
December a rose whiter than the dreadful
blue hues of those August Winters alone
you saw the light in the passage
I could not see I want to travel with your
hands, I want to reach for the road with
your smile take me with you

herein Memphis where
lovers don't die where the rain
pours like Miles Davis playing in a Cafe
on and on I realize you are with me those
August Winters

no-more am I alone
you see those river lights in Memphis
I am un-tired awaiting your love
in this driveway, we call ocean blue
a sweetness only that could be you.

BLOOD OF CHRIST

To reach the blood of Christ
You have to sing like
A sequoia on fire
The redeemer
Knows the dance
Of your soul
To seek love
One must reconcile
With the word
Of life

WOMAN HAVE ME

Women are silent creatures
of immense omniscience
their bodies are throbbing a spectacular
identity, they're remarkable sidereal breasts
filled with picturesque air,

their essence
is the embodiment of a dying cosmos
their strength, is a vitality no one can
comprehend, yet their eyes are solaced
with a brilliant rectangle of starry cello
creeks, they're without rivers because
their love is a vacuum of sane poetic
turbulence, there's nothing more that can
be said,

their kisses partake
in the making of new experiences
yet as time divides their juniper
closets, their fragile paintbrushes
elucidate an ivory trillium they're
rawer than stone tin breath,

they're rawer
than a love which is unbalanced
yet they're always consuming primrose

curtains, women are godly gentle nimble
tenderly moonlit, and they're rich with
eloquent emotion, they're not objects
of gamble, they're not objects at all they're
formlessly loved by music,

I'm spaced
out by the way their veracious sylphlike
canopy of bejeweled ember trees.
women are significant because they
bend, and unbend language like it's
a delicacy, yet I anticipate their
divine ornamentation of cataract
fleshy breasts, I'm lost in their
incommunicable bespangled gaze.
and in the end women have me.

DISBELIEF

Chrome velvet skies
your knees enveloped
 in silver seas your neck
 like a Vivaldi song you
call my heart and we
 have our hearts caught
in a lonely English Oak,
I love your maple fire you
of pine needle trees of
wine lost in disbelief,
you set my mind free.

GONE

empty bedroom taking the
keys, walking out alone.
I've slept on park benches
before, smelt the morning
rise, drank whiskey, looked upon
the stars, shaking my fists
saying "why did you've to
take her God", I remember
rolling around in the frost
nearly having hyperthermia,
I knelt down to the heavens
asked why? Oh, why me?
No reply, I drank more
whiskey, it takes time
for grief, if
only life wasn't the thief.
Like a piano each day
has a different melody
and we try to stick in
tune with the chord
of reality, sometimes
that chord is pain
and happiness.

ABERNATHY FOREST

In the Abernathy Forest
we belong, where the
oak trees grow tall and long
and the weather never
feels wrong, let's
travel back to the shire
where we belong cause
this world is such a callus
gong. Mountains are wounds to
the eyes, swords to soul
great is the valor of
battle, spear and arrows
fly high beyond the dragons
cry. for poetry is the pen tipped
in ink, skulls and dead bodies
grow upon halls of insecurity
Golden gates to the Dark Mage's
Stronghold a Celtic fable,

BLUE SWAN

Blue swan
feathers
 cinnamon
sunshine
orchestral goodbyes
like an Appalachian
mountain climb you
 surrender your
 flowered legs, and entwine
 with the gorgeous
melody of knowing
how our lyrics survived
 the longest lies

NAKED

All the grief
in the world is
dancing you to
the bluffs where
our tenderness will
hear the rhapsodies
of Emily Dickinson
scintillating across
the deep blueness of
our being where
our water is the
tapestry of solace

WAITING

Waiting for
a rose to bloom
is like waiting
 for your eyes to
 resume our soul's
 youth

BLUE CAT

The city was
bright and the desk
 was overflowing
with books there was a
blue cat on the
couch an incandescent woman asleep
beside me, paradise solitude,
no aloofness no horror
 I keep turning
the pages and have
 been melted by the
synchronicity of a
 mellow grace
this is admirable it is
 lovely it is a
passage to an
otherworldly
dwelling it is paradise
I shall consume
literature I shall
be
like a blue cat

INVERNESS

The chorus
 of red sea rain
slept on your velvet
 dress lovingly a gift
of unspoken fresh
life a starlit lyrebird
chirping it's joy-filled with
 breath the hearthside
purring charmingly your
eyelashes are a
wonder that could
 topple a whole army
you are the silence
 I'm chasing in a book
that beauty that shall forever
 hook the crimson lines of shadows in
my hill in the highlands in
 Inverness my
 only true God-given rest.

PASSION

Passion in love
is the involvement
 of the spirit renewing your life.
Passion consequently
frequents your life.
You must gaze, and
eye the earth in its
simple beauty not in
the fires of society,
 but in the fires of
your own virtues in
your own beauties
seek passion above all
else. It'll intensify your mind,
and make you kind.

TORN

torn cigarettes an
eclipse of regret the tide
moonlighted blue
hazy the gods are kind
and lazy the sweat of
forgotten dreams and
whiskey so poignant
I can breathe the
 withering soaked bloodshot
maples an oaky cloud
 of violet velvet
wounds and you pretend to be Bob
Dylan trying to wear
 David Bowie's clothes
 and you saturate
my sinew with the wisdom
of Rumi and there is
an opening in the
 tunnel the light
remains with our
raindrop hearts of Jupiter
dancing in our arms of
gorgeous beaches drenched in your
allure in your holy
 kiss of a song amiss.

EUGOWRA

Bushranger country-land
eucalyptus and red gums
smother the dry oily grass
wombats pass on the way
to Forbes, the Central West
is a glimpse of sunny warm
light, wide open spaces
white cypress like an ocean
of white delight, kangaroos
pounce & jump over the
barbed wire electrical
fences, cattle trotting
on, down the old road
bends. Broken rocks, old graveyards
where the dead are sleeping
quietly, gorge caves
the Lachlan open Murray
Cod hiding
in the under growth of
algae, catching golden
perch, eating and consuming
that for lunch you'd feel
a part of the river shrine
cause the country of
my ancestors is
in my blood,
I'm aboriginal

this is ingrained
in my heart.
I feel connected
one time sat under
the stars in Coonabarabran
soaking up the primordial
cosmic rays, my soul was
in the rainbow serpent
story, I'm a rainbow
warrior of the Bobroi
South Coogee
this my Ara Irititja
in Pitjantjatjara
old language
of the Anangu
Uluru
for this is my
story my life
we've many
people but
I believe in one
Australian
tribe

PERFIDIOUS

the perfidious
blue hazy whiskey lily,
macabre and tender
eviscerated and numbed
our mirth we of
sad rain and delirium
unabashed and
crepuscular the
dawn is where we
vex the tragedy of being

I FORGOT ABOUT HEMINGWAY

Numbed by the numberless dark
and besotted by the arrogance
of being overworked
by the heavens, skylarks
dancing in naked salt lakes
floating on a jarred fog of
silly sonnets
a growing myriad of
worthless novels buried
underneath the baroque
macabre nooks of the bookshelf
owned by the wit of Gertrude
Stein, Ezra Pound made out with
Zelda Fitzgerald, the book said
and Scott was whoring his
boxing gloves to Hemingway
the bulls of Spain were harrowed
savaged by the negligence
of Nabokov,
poetry does not
have to make sense of beauty
nor does it adhere to reason
there is a cat who is where
the sun grows old of humanity's
pursuit of a victory over

death, art somehow brings us
to the confessional where Faulkner
is ready to listen.

RED BIRD

We ranted about
absurdism and Kafkaesque
dreams, but we wanted
a Johnny Cash song
to make sense of this
squalid unknown
a sanctimonious song of
bare bones of raw stress
and glow oh darling you
have it all New York
and Venice at your heels
a sensuous scintillating
Red Bird
pouring reason into my
bones.

THE VIRGINS OF VIRGINIA

It was the blood moon and the normal activities were on eating the flesh of elders in the forest. Cutting off people's toes and dangling them off the sycamores. This was commonplace practice under the silhouette of the blood harvest. Churches embroiled with priests teeth glued to the altar. The Virgins of Virginia will be sacrificed in the forest again. God knows what happens there the flesh of kindred darkness hovers like a blue crimson spectre. Hopeless nights the wayfarers would wonder along the rivulet banks fishing out virgin breasts to eat, they like to smother the Virgins of Virginia. The feast would be rapturous, and the essence of the cool air would constrict their skin making them paler for hell but they would be impaled sincerely, and miraculously the pool of shadows in its power would impose beauty on the void of the drifted midnight. The incubus awaits the Virgins. The farmers would carry them after shooting them pile their bodies on the ancient draft horse cart and they'd be driven through the bog and the mist would consume their souls. Memories of persistent pain arouses their priestly hearts.

Part Two The Altar

The backyard of the catholic priest's yard was filled with decaying tissue from last night's slaughter, meat cleavers piled upon meat cleavers heads, and endless rows of fermenting intestines wreathed on the apple tree and an altar encompassing prayer for the Lord.

"Our father in heaven
forgive us for we have not
killed enough in your name

let the blood flow like
a great batch of Atlantic
salmon let the blood
water the soil with
the tears of despair let
this holy covenant of
shame, and sanctimonious
suffering be your grain
heaven, let their hearts
rain in terror let this slaughter
be your communion my
Holy Ghost."

There was no resentment in how things were done, this was the Lord's gift a sacrifice of beautiful honesty. And their blood was, and is a language of purity, for many a man

tried to let their desires weigh down, but the man of the Lord wouldn't let his desire to kill weigh down, for the endless darkness was a crucifying party. And the demons stained the the lawns of heaven with blood, oh blessed is the sacrifice said priest Ravenberry, "For it is prettiest dandelion in all of existence." His martyrs were a herd of unintelligent souls; broken men. The priest had to do the lords will and that was to slaughter all the virgins before the sun set, and so he did with his hoard of dead men ex murdered his malice, and vice were perfect in the eyes of heaven; heaven being hell.

SONGBIRDS IN MIAMI

Hear the ocean springs the junipers
they swear in sync of courage
bestowed in your gorgeous clothes
your academic toes of morning glories
and lilacs waking up early the eastern
starling dances in vein waiting for the
August rain, blood against timber
sweat against love sinew heavens
flesh dances in sync of sunny Greek
fleece, and jackets made in Miami
stink, oh come winter where the songbirds
are awake again where we'll dance with
the westerly ting where Southern Comfort
calls us into arms, and plums are spread
across the farms, and harvest feels like
December Jazz in a funny
calm like James Baldwin's charm.

THE SEAFARER WHO SAW DEATH

The gentle breeze of the English sun shuns the rain-softened sands of the Dorset shore. The easterly winds were philharmonic, and you could feel the glow on your skin like a renascent angel that would caress your skin The rain acted like a beckon for the divine heavens. A storm was coming. It was preceding from the north of Ireland, and I could feel it choking me subconsciously. I could feel it arousing my senses, and my bones were scattered luminous like a book never read and kept under a bed. I opened the book, "The Sea Farer Who Saw Death."

The old man wheelbarrowed his sorrow to the crimson cliffs of Dorset, unafraid and aloof. His love was the freshness of the sea and the mysteries that were caked into each flow of the torrent. The old man stared at the stateless sea, wondering what the purpose was of each current, without any line hooks for the fish that he would accumulate for dinner. What was the purpose? He thought these crucial existential thoughts tumbled around his head like clothes in a tumble dryer.

Every day, the old man would go to the beach and stare at the ocean, patiently waiting for a sign from anything, but no sign ever appeared as the years passed; still, the man, tense with the explosiveness of not knowing himself, pursued the ocean to give him answers, but nothing happened .Nobody came, nothing awash, nothing adrift, just the decadence of silence and the diaphanous Dead Sea snakes accumulated upon the shore. An ominous stir was amidst the pains of his existence. He'd gather seeds for his garden that was fathered by his family for generations, and the sun would be kind some days and terrible other days. He had a cat, and the cat would follow him to the shore awaiting a call, but nothing happened.

Only rain and the swiftness of doubt pursued his broken, untouchable heart, which was drawn to the sea in search of answers; answers that we all seek but never receive. More and more, the man realised that there were more answers that were invisible He stared into the water, and the water purposed a reflection for the old man. He saw that nature needs no answers to living, nor does it need a purpose for credulity. Nature is answerless. But then the sea surreptitiously answered the man. The sea spiraled into a torrent and a piano floated playing Rachmaninoff's Rhapsody on a Theme of Paganini. The sea catapulted a letter to the Old Man

A Letter From Pari In August 1943 When Germany Occupied Paris

To my dear friend William Chaberworth:

I have sent you a letter of my feelings. Something that is discernable and is quite frankly ranked a sweet aroma from my heart. As you know, the Nazis have Pari, but I thought I'd send you one last letter.

I've attempted to understand your way of feeling your truth in the darkness by the way it is raining in Paris. I cannot understand your toiling in the squalidness of hope that I might come back again so that we might pursue our arranged marriage I am here to help the wounded. I peer out the window and it is raining in Pari and its endless stream pelts the ground. It's endless. I cannot help but think of you and your nets hanging out in the water waiting for a fresh catch. I cannot help but remember our times I am reading Charlotte Bronte I cannot help it, and I wonder if I existed in another universe, would I not be where I am now? I cannot fathom the allegory of the rain, or what you want, yet there is nothing like this anxiety. There is nothing beyond it.

And yet I love it more than myself. Its dangerousness I can feel in every sinew of my body. Your unendingly marvelous frailty. I feel in the cold, cruel, decadent wind as I stroll the streets of Pari. I feel this utter contempt for human life and I'm drawn to it like a badger is drawn to its hole I love your cynicism. Its melody is lacquered on the coffee-colored wallpaper of my study. Your breath in the dust that is flowing tentatively, and I rescind the fact that you are no more. I have to reach this zenith. I have to be endowed by the emptiness you have left for me. Unwillingly, I wish to set out into the rain without remorse, and without feeling. I welcome the rivulets and the expansiveness of sorrow. I welcome the rivulets and the expansiveness of sorrow. I welcome the rivulets and the expansiveness of sorrow.

Oh, this rain is feverish and obstinate. I have come to meet you, dear rain, and I shall read in silence and be with the books that wish to be with me. If only Atlas held up all the books that mattered, and the earth crumbled into the abyss, the words would exist, permeating beyond time. I do think of you every day and every moment, but a wakeful nightmare is something I cannot put my finger on. Something transient is with me. Something that is beyond both of us Nobody is infatuated by war. I am utterly miserable. I see the sky bloodied and ignited with hatred. I am a slave. And as you know, I am a Jew. I have to hide. You know it. I know it. The SS troops are going to get me at some point. I have done incredibly well to hide my origins. And yet nothing else quenches my heart except the thought of this somehow reaching you beyond the armaments of horror I would do it so fast that we could walk the beaches of Dorset once more as we did in the summer of 1937. Oh how I wish to hold your body against mine. This terrible yearning for you cannot be left unsaid. I love you as mightily and strongly as anyone could. I hope I make it for both of our sakes.

BROWN SUGAR

thighs sullied in
brown sugar
melodies of glass
breasts brandished in
port wine, our kisses are cocoa
a sensuous anthem of
nakedness where God
is not allowed where
a church is covered in
red lingerie your sins are
my hunger for a room filled
with grateful candlelight
a montage of Casablanca
better than the Tuscan sun
red dried tomatoes in a stir-fry
oh love is delicious when you
are making poetry with vanilla extract.

ART OF THE DARK

the silence dances off
your lips the rain swallows
your body whole your flesh
is anew, your whispers kiss
me into the truth, I have seen
the alone void, the voices forgotten
your eyelashes turn me into a lilac
drifting into the evermore moonlight
you're awake, you're awake, the beauty
that you are is unquenchable
beyond the truth beyond the
beating of a fading heart
stuck in the middle of that raindrop
in England, you see me for who I am
a fading melody
a fading star the fading
art of the dark.

ASPHODEL RISEN

You were entitled to my chest in the rain, and when the darkness came, your arms were spread all over my flesh. I wondered if I was entitled to your breasts as they fucked me out of this line, your legs wrapped around mine, your voice shaking me like a drug out of time.Your orgasms destroyed the meaninglessness I faced, and as a result, I felt your warmth and tenderness. You annihilated my manhood. You took away my misery. Your vagina was the unsinkable love. I tasted you when the fears of this world surrounded me. A truthful lilac you are.

I want to cause you sweet clitoral damage with a melody that you can only understand that no man could try. It is in this warmth that the moonlight that bounces off your skin like a black swan that endows me with this feisty, tempestuous rush of uncertainty that holds my arms and takes away what tries to hold me down into decay. The darkness was aplenty, the rigamarole lovely, unlike the clandestine hopes of other men. Your lips personified me and put me in a place above the brutalities of the half-witted masses. I hoped for nothing less than to see your hair radiate in the rain of Paris that kept me in the alleyways. It is beautiful nausea to hold you down amidst the lilies of creation.

Salt peppered cheeks Have you not noticed the resin on your cheeks that rescinds into the darkness? Have you heard of the Bordeaux snow or the wonders of lost Spartan pottery shards?Or the discouraged opaque mist that reappears in the contrasting myths of our symbolic natures.Oh history, I've seen a lot of blood and no love but that of a kiss that transcends the timelessness of forgiveness.

Agonizingly sweet hair dripping wet from the saccharine air of Helsinki, gorgeous, nimble, god awful brilliant. Women, I thought, are the keepers of feelings thatched in the decay of a deadened song, written in the isles of Mount Vesuvius where Nietzsche was once said to stand, glaring at the malted land. Courage, it seems, is invariably a part of our natures, registered in the essences of our loneliness, that love would somehow triumph over death. Freeness was an unwritable feeling, a Jungian response to existence; this feeling was unrelenting, a smothering of nothingness, preserving the suffocation from which the nothingness had emerged.Our duty is to be poetic trespassers paralysed by an unknowable myth that we ascertain, feel, and our hunger for nothingness grows complacent amidst the dust we are returning to. Forever is an unsayable God, and love, love, love, love, is uncontainable, neurotically indispensable, and oh love suffocates me.

I'd rather talk about the luminosity of a star. I'd rather talk about the shapes of blue, green, and tinted shells. I'd rather talk about a metaphor so extemporaneous that it'd make your socks turn into feathers. I'd rather explore the euphoria we experience from the image of damaged sandstone. I'd rather watch your feathers touch an old pipe in the bay that's covered in algae. I'd rather have that than death. Love is merely concrete action. People break up because their partners weren't good enough to continue the relationship. If you're a shitty boyfriend, you're a shitty actor. Love is operatic imitation. Love is irrational theater. Romeo was a good romantic. He could lie and be an ingenious charlatan. Because in love, we're all charlatans and mystics.

I'd rather spend a billion unknown centuries trying to understand why you left me in the street cold, without a blanket, cold without your graceful neck. I'd rather spend a century wondering why you didn't yearn to kiss me savagely and barbarically. I'd rather that than be left alone in the valley of wake-less souls. I'd rather you be the philosophy I died over. I'd like that more than anything. I'd rather see your wet, rainy breasts shut out the sun than spend an age in a coffin pondering in unifying suspense as to why you wouldn't be infatuated with me. I'd rather break the language of 24 coffins, 24 elegies than to feel alone. Only you, darling, could help me know. I'd rather leave myself to fund a contribution to the heaven's incense of your extravagant lit dew.

Our hegemonic traditions are based on outdated and unnecessary virtues. In this accepted morality, race, culture, class, our symbolic attitudes towards these further highlight the much needed facilitated values that have in unison provided humanity with a chance of survival, that being love, kindness, forgiveness, any faculty that yields the power of divulging what can be said in the Nietzschean dialect. Change happens when we reprimand such values that edify our hunger for control. In this love all, there is a sweetness enduring the decadence of this undefinable song we call life Asphodel Risen.

ADORN

The Light adorns
your love Seeking
the duty of grace By
 enamouring the
 disgrace
 We are only human
to marry your marrow
 As Dionysus would
say Is the duty of being a man?
Seasons perish I was alone.
 Your French kiss
remains Stronger than
the tears Of mankind
Beauty is portrayed in
your dress Evermore
we are reunited in shame
 Only love, only the sound of love
Is here your arms
wrenching my Heart's mistakes

GETHSEMANE

your neck is
Gethsemane's wild
 lonesome wind
you take every
 sun rained drop
and make my soul
covered in the oxygen of
 grace, of mountainous delight
my lady you sing
 sinew into melody
into the tumultuous
shadows of Lord
Byron of junipers on fire a
 storm of forever blue.

BREACH

You got all
of my sweat in
your back pocket
 you got all the
moonlight above your knees
 and you corner my
despair with how
 your lips make New
York glow, alone
no more, you
enchant and my
absent mind your
escape is all those
conversations we
had in the rain at
long beach let's
breach the darkest
storm with a song
 of puddled snow

MITTEN THE TABBY

To see a
 big tabby rolling
 around in the shrub
face towards me
hissing with a beautiful
scent of I don't give a
 fuck is paradise his long
tail in the hair his
mane unmolested he is
 a God and here I am
wishing I had the life of
him to not care to go
from place to place
without a thought
 or care is what I
consider heaven he
 is wretchedly unique
a mist of nature I
want to know the most

FOUR KITTENS

The neighborhood is
 quiet and there is a
fading purple rainstorm in the distance
 Here I am with four
 kittens in my forties aloof content,
existentially at peace with
 myself they slumber on my
fat belly as I write
 my very next poetry
collection the
pavement outside
 is littered with dead
 sparrow bones my
 boys like to play
and when they
play the rip the
 natural world on its
 toes we don't care
what happens now
everything is distanced
everything is transient except this love
 that lies on my belly like
 purgatory worth
praising such is the
the beauty of the purr
always warming the

anxious depths
of the belly always healing
the pit of
non-existence within me

SOLITUDE IN LOVE

Solitude in love is the evocation of serenity. When you are in love, and you require solitude the greatest implication of peace is to allow solitude to happen. Solitude in love is the greatest kind of love. Solitude is the allowance of time it does not mean being apart from each other. It means being together in unity, it means that your time is important to you and that your existence is your own. It means that your time to yourself is important it is respecting someone else's time to have their own subjective experience.

Our society is built on the ideology of taking everybody's time we have to work we have to pay the mortgage we are our time is always being taken away by someone or somebody because their time is more important than the breath you are given. You are given one body.

Human beings die every day it is the natural course of life. But our moments live on forever. To give your time up for someone else is heroic, and love is heroic. But we also must allow other people to have their own poems, paintings, and dances.

Tomorrow could be your fatality. But this moment that we are given is ours. Love at times is about giving other people the time to write their own poems, and paintings. Let us remember the power of solitude. How can you facilitate the truth of love by giving away someone else's solitude? It is not the hermit part of solitude that I am talking about. It is the respect for someone else to write their own existence for a moment.

DOORS OF PERCEPTION

The doors of heaven
are open
to your hands.
the sky yearns
to inhale
the perfume
of your smile,
the aromatic
essence of your
sunshine. there
are doors open
to your chorus
of perception.

SONNET OF DEATH

Shadows wear love above growing death
silence enters the womb of doves breath
love is the victory over our heart's nest
the angels wicked in love glow forever sown
entailing your wounds of bells duties blown
the wicked armors of voice storms forget
you have seen the page filled with regret
you forget shadows become your rest
lyrics spoken in night joy, bathed in a bayou
sorrowed demons upon your breath
follow your misery today upon your lay
forgive me, forgive us forgive death today
for no love can quench the thirst of our earth.

STILL

To where we
sat in
despair
to where
we sat in tune
to the wild orchids
that grew into our veins
we stare again

in wonderment of
what is to be
where silence
stills our knees.

SEE

we
indulged
the sea air
and I kissed
your neck as you saw
the sprawl of mountainous
fog, effulging
attraction
to what stood
before elven
song and mercy
takes us.

BROOKLYN

There was sudden ecstasy in the air, your tender voluptuous legs crossed and sweet. We were having coffee in an obscure cafe in Brooklyn. It was raining in Brooklyn, and we had bought all the books we needed for the rainy season for the marvelous chestnut bookshelf we had just purchased from an antique restoration store.

The light was translucent, and it bounced off Margaret's shoulders diaphanously. Margaret toyed with the idea of living in seclusion in a remote village somewhere near the Himalayas. Pass me some sugar please dear! Don't you think it would be lovely if we lived in the rainforest away from society, and just lived out the rest of our days in harmony with nature?

And you could write the book you are always talking about writing. And I could grow my hair long and you could have a beard like some Georgian orthodox monk.

Don't you think it would be great to retreat? I do think it is a good idea dear, but we have to live realistically, and I think for the moment the best escape we have is our books, and perhaps we will make a trip up there at some point. We should always follow the rain. I believe in that as a prayer. The rain started to slow down, and I kissed her on the cheek and said let's go and disappear like the rain.

DON'T THINK

The sun is uninviting today it is
Like any other day
Absurd and inundated
with the worst kind of shadows
You are a seeker of validation
Spending your time videoing yourself
using a hula hoop to climb above
The ranks of culture, and popularity
You are not the worst of all the looneys
You do read the latest Rupi Kaur book and
In your spare time you think intellectual
Masturbation is Ben Shapiro raging on about
How transgenders are not women, don't think
You have let the internet do the thinking
For you, surviving is easy all you've to
Do is call UberEats, and the right assortment
Of gourmet burgers come to your doorsteps
You don't think, you are on autopilot
Endlessly watching the crazed cesspool
Of instagram with its torrents of photos
And instagram models yearning to be the
Next Kendall Jenner, you are bombarded
with responses from tweets saying you
Are wrong, Donald Trump is the best
President of all time he is nearly
Better than Abraham Lincoln, but
You are drowning in information

THE goal of learning is not always
To be informed but it is to
Be smart enough to let go of things
That essentially don't matter
Because in the end the time you
Waste is the time you
Wish you had saved.

PHONE CALL

It's December again. I missed your call. I thought that you would call me today. I thought I'd get 10 messages from you saying how much you missed me. But no, you're dead.

You died in my arms in the hospital. I know that we've been separated by life and death right now.
I remember our times on the beach, dancing; our moments reading Baudelaire; those moments looking at the beautiful ocean and the sprawling darkness that devoured our emotions.

I thought you would call me. I have to wait for you all this time. The cats meow again. I thought you would call me. I wake up and go to the bookstore, and I feel that you will appear somehow.

But no, you died. And in my grief, I imagine a world that is fictionalised, fictionalised by your beauty and your kisses that devoured me when we first met at that cafe, but I lost it.
I lost you in the mess of existence. I miss you. Would you call me? Somehow you might call me, I don't know. Maybe it will happen. Let's see.

NIGHTFALL

Her sycamore, dahlia, coloured dress sparkled dangerously in an indelible dark I fell in love with the gross starriness of her being. The city was a prowling, sprawling mess of tired human beings living for dimes; the only real poverty is not knowing one's own real dreams and realising that at an old age is hell on earth. Purposeful movement is found in the dark, and the reason many human beings are lost in such a dark is that they won't take the risk to peer out into that entrenching dark.

Nightfall arrived it was our disposition our wanderings that brought us to the cold difficultly lit stark woods. A rivulet ran afresh through the middle of the mad dark oaks, we were acquainted with the terrible aloneness a symbolic silence eluded us it depicted us as lonesome, and we are bound to its blood to its calling forevermore

There was no love or pathway out it was just the darkness that ennui the melancholy sweeping our veins and I vomited out our sorrow poetically, nonetheless, I found myself in this ruination I found myself at the end of all things.
I actively went on a whim to go more afoot through the terrifically stretching darkness elastic in spirit grotesque inwardly. I wallowed at my misery I reflected on my insignificance and contemplated that this is human to be yourself only yourself really yourself whence the darkness arrived from.

BLACK SUN

Officer Grayson son that's my name, put your hands on the windshield you piece of shit. I'm gonna suture your anus to the walls of the cell and you ain't gonna get out son you are lucky to even be breathing now lad.

The sun was faint and Grayson loves shooting a black, he bathes in the misery of the negro, little did he know that the young delinquent had a father on the force, and Grayson would not only get the beating of his life he's going to be thrown into the water with the rest of white men who think that slavery should be still a part of modern society.

Billy was a young student from Detroit, athletic, and morally good a kind kid who never did the world any harm. Billy tried to volunteer his time to take care of old men suffering from dementia. To Billy life was not about race, gender, or ethnicity life was about making the right choices and he could feel the echo of the wind shrouding his soul as Grayson ripped uppercuts into his ribs, Billy didn't try to fight it he wasn't like that he was a good kid.

JOHNNY AND THE MOON

"You'll be something one day. Johnny the Moon will be proud of you. "Remember when he told you those Nam stories, the guns and utter starvation, he made it through it," my Mom said before she died of cancer, leaving me poor with no estate, no name to put on my pocket, no wealth or start.The future is bright for the youth of this planet. The future is bright for smart, intelligent, informed people. Nothing could be further from the truth. A world of intelligence means jack-shit. It means nothing. Life is squalid, life is irrecoverably senseless, and the only sense that can come out of such a fear-manifested maelstrom is love. Love is not further from the truth, yet when you get it, it is a rare moment of surreptitious, or serendipitous, you might say.

I once read in a book, or maybe it was said in my dreams, that the more shit you shovel, and the more shit you can take, the better things will come to those who don't break. Maybe that was some sort of cathartic tale. A pigeon who was golden in a world of decay, a flightless bird that could fly. Maybe that is bullshit poetry, as I drank another glass of whiskey staring at the faceless road. There was not even a scent of joy when I stared at it.

The road stretched northwards. I had nothing in my backpack but a gun and my bottle of Ballentine's Whiskey. I thought a man could go crazy walking for miles on not even a farm to find a job, just meaningless territory with no horses, no rams, not even a steer to look at, no birds, just a sky of ravenous torture. I suppose I'd go on forwards, but contemplation is the problem. All I did was overthink the territory and that stabbed me. I had to philosophise everything, even the bare ass fucked sun. The more I thought about it, the worse it got.

Life is a fucked-up road, intangible at times, brilliant, at times sophisticated, at times sexed up, at times pointless, like the ending of most sentences. The thing is, the start of a sentence is the juice, the middle of it, especially the clauses, is the magic, the full stop, like life is euthanasia. As long as I went northwards, as long as I kept moving, there was a job for me out there, and if I stood looking at the ground, I'd never sleep, I'd never wake up to reality. Because moving forward is the only reality.

TENDERISE

as I sink deeper
into tragedy
as I soliloquise
shadow and melancholy,
my foggy mind
sees a twig dancing
alone in a deep
divine and I think
of how your hands
tenderise my doom
and conjure my bloom.

HOBART IS SCOTLAND

Decanted wine, sorting through old photos of Orange. Moving swiftly away from trepidation in a town I always almost felt lost in. The sun is a route to a promised land. Where the moonlight is jaded by the meow of a cat. Leaving behind everything I deemed valuable, I eyed my own new destiny. Every time I went, it felt like I was looking at pictures of the Tweedsmuir river in Scotland on Google Images.The wild bliss of forgotten stones, the primordial symbology of the wind. Driftwood ashore, Tasmania is Scotland, at least to me. I assumed that my journey would be indifferent to myself. As a struggling twenty-year-old, I did not know what I wanted to really do. I sighed a great deal. There is poetry in this struggle, a fortune to be told. A cheek to be kissed, a story to be held. My life is the sum of choices, as we all understand.

Often, we underestimate where the weather is taking us. Or what kind of rose is going to be up in the morning tomorrow? We ascertain a certain, yet subtle song within ourselves. Am I good enough to exist? I feel disenfranchised, dislocated somewhere in my soul. Could I write? Am I able to write the unwritable? To articulate things I thought I'd never be able to do. Listen to a woman, and love her dearly. The absence of myself, the piles of cigarette ashes, the despondency associated with the negligence of my own nature. I thought maturity was waking up in the morning, and looking forward to what was possible; escaping the impossible. I thought failure was bad, and yet every miracle in life has been associated with some kind of failure or loss. The mesmerising truth that is the rain comes in troves to let you know that you aren't alone at all.

Am I worthy of the morning? Can the moonlight articulate itself to me? I am barely breathing. As I write this, the ominous voices have me at bay. Delectable neglect, negation, negation, repetition in my mind. I have a soft spot for Scotland. Tasmania got me with its endless winter rains and morning cold. Frost is deeper than the universe. I am fascinated with Mount Wellington and its mystical rhythms I am ebbing from a viewpoint at work in Kingston. I am inspired by its murkiness and its ghostliness. I call Tasmania "the jewel of the Celtic Isles. The rain visits me, and I visit it in my steel cap boots.

I journeyed here for a safe haven. A place where the words run wild, milk, honey in the rivulet track, and Blackmans Bay, its name makes me think of Joseph Conrad's ship. Unspoken love, unbeknownst groves of truth. I have seen the lonely streets of wayward nature, but in Hobart I have seen Scotland everywhere I go. from looking out the window. I walked on the shores of Long-Beach. I have been to Scotland. I have been there. The inseparable beast of Scotland permeates all who come here. For everyone who has been to Scotland, they have pierced the cathedrals, and the echelons of malady are so intoxicating that you are desirous of all that is within the tracks of Mount Wellington. The cats call you by name; imagination; William Blake clouds. There is a drought of ugliness Hobart in all its glory is Scotland; linger and consume, and let that truth edify your soul.In love, women, the beaches. The cold brings its own ghosts, apparitions of melody. In all its beauty, a hymn is made, and continuously remade.

No other writer wouldn't see Hobart as Sydney because Sydney does not have mountains that transcend time. It is no sweeter than a Willie Smith's Apple Cider. Hobart nights are pristine, almost elucidating. I am not here to advertise its beauty, but to present the case that Hobart itself created a Scotland within me. Nowhere else have I felt freer and transcendental like Henry Thoreau David's novel Walden to quote

Thoreau on that, "I wanted to live deep and suck out all the marrow of life." I am the sunniest when the cats prance and prattle with my soul. I have been to places only Walt Whitman would have dreamed of. Mount Wellington, with its harsh cold, God-given face of tangible beauty, relents in its efforts to entice me with love.Of all the stories to be told, and beauty to be beheld. I am an insufferable vent like the murals of Picasso. If you could only see the freedom in the mountainous nature of Hobart, would you be able to see the spirit of Joseph Conrad's ship illustrating the invisible Scotland right before your eyes?

Nothingness can drown you, but beauty can forestall death. I was sent here as a nomad, a conqueror of myself. To pursue a journey to write a story that would stifle your mind. I want you to see and eat Scotland, from the generosity of the Salamanca Grocer to the old lady you have to help through the door. There are metaphors written on the walls of Centrepoint for the gracefulness of St David's Cathedral. John Keats lived here. Poetry lives here, and its force makes men crumble in forgiveness. My life changed by just looking at the mist wrapping and swerving undulatingly around the breast of Mount Wellington. Here my soul had changed it had said, "Here become who you are not who you think you but what the mist is within you." In the sweetness, in the aether of this messy, hungering, gunslinging love. The mist will make you its own child. I am a child of that mist. Decanted wine, sorting through old photos of Orange. Moving swiftly away from trepidation in a town I always almost felt lost in. The sun is a route to a promised land. Where the moonlight is jaded by the meow of a cat. Leaving behind everything I deemed valuable, I eyed my own new destiny. Every time I went, it felt like I was looking at pictures of the Tweedsmuir river in Scotland on Google Images.The wild bliss of forgotten stones, the primordial symbology of the wind. Driftwood ashore, Tasmania is Scotland, at least to me. I assumed that my journey would be indifferent to myself. As a struggling twenty-year-old, I did not know what I wanted to really do. I sighed a great deal. There is poetry in this struggle, a fortune to be told.

A cheek to be kissed, a story to be held. My life is the sum of choices, as we all understand.

Often, we underestimate where the weather is taking us. Or what kind of rose is going to be up in the morning tomorrow? We ascertain a certain yet subtle song within ourselves. Am I good enough to exist? I feel disenfranchised, dislocated somewhere in my soul. Could I write? Am I able to write the unwritable? To articulate things I thought I'd never be able to do. Listen to a woman, and love her dearly. The absence of myself, the piles of cigarette ashes, the despondency associated with the negligence of my own nature. I thought maturity was waking up in the morning, and looking forward to what was possible; escaping the impossible. I thought failure was bad, and yet every miracle in life has been associated with some kind of failure or loss. The mesmerising truth that is the rain comes in troves to let you know that you aren't alone at all.

Am I worthy of the morning? Can the moonlight articulate itself to me? I am barely breathing. As I write this, the ominous voices have me at bay. Delectable neglect, negation, negation, repetition in my mind. I have a soft spot for Scotland. Tasmania got me with its endless winter rains and morning cold. Our frost is deeper than the universe. I am fascinated with Mount Wellington and its mystical rhythms ebbing from a viewpoint at work in Kingston. I am inspired by its murkiness and its ghostliness. I call Tasmania "the jewel of the Celtic Isles. The rain visits me, and I visit it in my steel cap boots.

I journeyed here for a safe haven. A place where the words run wild, milk, honey in the rivulet track, and Blackmans Bay, its name makes me think of Joseph Conrad's ship. Unspoken love, unbeknownst groves of truth. I have seen the lonely streets of wayward nature, but in Hobart, I have seen Scotland everywhere I go. from looking out the window. I walked on the shores of Long Beach. I have been to Scotland. I have been there. The inseparable beast of Scotland permeates all who come here.

To everyone who has been to Scotland, they have pierced the cathedrals, and the echelons of malady are so intoxicating that you are desirous of all that is within the tracks of Mount Wellington. The cats call you by name; imagination; William Blake clouds. There is a drought of ugliness Hobart in all its glory is Scotland; linger and consume, and let that truth edify your soul.In love, women, the beaches. The cold brings its own ghosts, apparitions of melody. In all its beauty, a hymn is made and continuously remade.

No other writer wouldn't see Hobart as Sydney because Sydney does not have mountains that transcend time. It is no sweeter than a Willie Smith's Apple Cider. Hobart nights are pristine, almost elucidating. I am not here to advertise its beauty, but to present the case that Hobart itself created a Scotland within me. Nowhere else have I felt freer and transcendental like Henry Thoreau David's novel Walden to quote Thoreau on that, "I wanted to live deep and suck out all the marrow of life." I am the sunniest when the cats prance and prattle with my soul. I have been to places only Walt Whitman would have dreamed of. Mount Wellington, its harsh, cold, God-given face of tangible beauty, relents to coax me with love. Of all the stories to be told, and beauty to be beheld. I am an insufferable vent like the murals of Picasso. If you could only see the freedom in the mountainous nature of Hobart, would you be able to see the spirit of Joseph Conrad's ship illustrating invisible Scotland right before your eyes?

Nothingness can drown you, but beauty can forestall death. I was sent here as a nomad, a conqueror of myself. To pursue a journey to write a story that would stifle your mind. I want you to see and eat Scotland, from the generosity of the Salamanca Grocer to the old lady you have to help through the door. There are metaphors written on the walls of Centrepoint for the gracefulness of St David's Cathedral. John Keats lives here. Poetry lives here, and its force makes men crumble in forgiveness. My life changed by just looking at the mist wrapping and swerving undulatingly around the breast of Mount Wellington. Here my soul had changed it had said, "Here become who you are not who you think you but what the mist is within you." In the sweetness, in the aether of this messy, hungering, gunslinging love. The mist will make you its own child. I am a child of that mist.

BLOOM

This electrifying
feeling across
strange towns
that evaporates
me in an emblematic
song that can
cause no wrong
that sifts your heart
melds it strong
and we walk beyond
innocence and doom
and somewhere
surreptitious
we echo
and bloom.

GILGANDRA

I remember Gilgandra
air, and Dubbo moonlight
glazed by Mutawintji
sights
of ochre
caught in my
eyes beastly
and always
giving me
delight
of rhapsodic
divinity that
juicy
kiss
of history's
last sign
symbolic and
always mine.

NGURRBUL

The first
rains came
the emus were soaking
up the water in the
waterhole
and many kangaroos
were happy as you
sifting through the
dream time anew
like a silhouette
of two swamp wallabies
seeking you.

Wiradjuri noun: Ngurrbul means love and friendship in
Wiradjuri.

THE DIARY

I'm troubled you see. I've an illness, I believe she exists in my shaking fingers and nowhere else. I feel lonely, but when I write her out I see the light somehow. I didn't know who she was, or where she existed. She knew me and I knew her somehow. I don't write for other people, I write for her. I write words about her and I cry with her as I see darkness. I wanted to know her name I thought If I wrote more she'd speak to me somehow. I didn't want to write egotistically our marriage was in those words, our children, our hope strength, future home. Our moments of happiness, dancing kissing hugging, sexual fantasies. Maybe we're the universe beginning and end, maybe when I die you die with all the stories I had to write about her for day on end. No one could comprehend I see no world except her brown eyes.

We were both madly obsessed with each other that's why we wrote about each other everyday since we're one life story. I had a theory that she was trapped in my poems, in my words in my pain somehow. I knew she loved me and I loved her, she revealed more of myself, every time. I write I see something of her in me and I in her, she is dead I'm dead to a dead poem, a dead word, I'm caged in poetry, I can't and will never escape I love her too much. I feel as though my breath walks up on my journal. I didn't know, I just didn't know why I had to enclose my soul into this diary. She was my wildest aroma, I had to eat her rose like figure all day, all night long for eternity. For it was her sweet green eyes that, made me go crazy beyond anything I've ever consumed.

No bottle of whiskey or wine could make me flee from those graceful jewels of heavens & oceans. Everything I've ever written was about her, no word could replace, no tongue, no experience; we both dread this world, we hate it. She wore a silk white dress and her body was dark chocolate, she was absolutely ethereal. It's a disorder madness beyond belief. I could write novels about her forever.

Maybe when I die I will end up in the poem with her writing more poems about our times together. Maybe one day I will meet her in real life. Her tears were my rain, her angry was thunder and lighting. I knew when it rained. I was doing something wrong, when It thundered I knew I had to write about her to make her happy. I don't know what this is, the world was always complicated. When I lay in bed wrestling with these thoughts of her and me.

STORY

Stories are very important to who we are. Stories, tell us who we are. Stories, show us who we are. Stories are essential to living a meaningful life. If you want to succeed in life. If you want to go beyond what you believe you are capable of.

You have to tell yourself the right story. You have to be the hero of your story. you have to go beyond the limitations of the crowd.

You have to say to yourself, I am capable and I am worthy of living my dreams I am capable of becoming, who I am supposed to be. And to have a meaningful relationship with life itself. You have to tell yourself the right story you have to feed your consciousness the right words, you have to feed your soul the right words. Think of life as a story or a novel. It is like a movie but you get to write it, and you are capable of writing yourself the right story. All you have to do is believe in yourself. The human imagination created everything in the material world.

When you walk out onto the street, the material world was created by people with ideas. The houses, the cars.

Everything you see around you that was made by mankind was created by an idea. It was sparked by creativity. It was influenced by passion and a drive to see life as more than just a series of events. At the centre of who you are is a story at the centre of who you are is a light at the centre of who you are supposed to be is a potential reality, there is a gateway into a realm of ideas and possibilities in you is the hope of a better world. In you is the innovative structure of being that has created and manifests itself in the world as a force for good.

You are capable of being that force for good. you're better than anyone else thinks of you. You are not other people's opinions. You are the light. When you think of the light, you think of a fire that never goes out, you are better than what everybody else makes you out to be. You are the universe in motion. You are gravity. You are the laws of physics. You have to have a mind over matter to get somewhere in life. You have to be able to see beyond the big dark ideas of groups. It is in you that the universe is capable of you. It is your intention to become a hero, do not live in the dark.

Do not let the crowd. Do not let the haters dictate who you are supposed, have faith and patience, it will help you in those days of darkness. Those days you do not want to go out of bed. Those days, you do not want to go to work those days you do not want to wash the dishes. Those days you do not want to even leave the house. You can get through it if you aim higher than the shadows that yearn to swallow you.

Love is the original power of the universe. Love is the power of God in motion. Love is the most important potion. You have to find the light, you have to find your mind. So, like I said because she was meaningful and you'll find God. But not only will you find God, but you'll also find yourself. You'll find the power, honesty, and integrity of the universe.

If you pursue what is meaningful, you will find that your mind and soul become connected you embody the power of the universe, you embody the energy of atoms neutrons anti-matter, and dark matter you embody the power of possibility. It's in your mind it's in your soul it's in your heart. There's poetry in this. There's poetry in arrival at a point in time where you are connected with the energy which formed everything.

The energy which formed everything is flowing through your veins. Remember that you're not small. You are the universe in action. Do not forget that fact.

What people get wrong a lot of the time, is that they follow the ideas of other people. They get sucked into the world of groups, they let their behavior, become influenced by the crowd. And there's quite a prominent problem with this scenario is that human beings were born to be individuals, but society predicates that we should be group thinkers.

And there is something deeply dangerous about this. You get lost in a fog of unmeaning. That's why people cannot find any meaningful purpose, because they're not willing to jump into the unknown, they're not willing to make that leap of faith into the cesspool of fire, which is the search for meaning. I think that's why people do not want to improve themselves. That's why they do not want to ever try something new, and that's why a lot of people are risk-averse. To go beyond that flaw that so many human beings have you'll have to find the story that you've been searching for.

LOVE IS THE GREATEST GIFT

Love is the greatest gift. When we talk about love, we often assign a certain value to it. We give love some images, and that's the problem.

When we fixate on an image of love, we endeavour to make love an object, we endeavour to make it a possession. But when we really let go of our desire to control the image and entity of love, we become aware of the truth that love is the value of freedom. Artists, musicians, poets, authors, philosophers, and scientists all do the same thing: they try and box up the energy of love I am guilty of doing this with my art. Love has meaning, and often there's this strange attraction to making love into something it's not. When we find love, we become its image, and its image is invisible. Love is the force beyond attraction.

Those who preach love must love as if it were a way of self-knowing. Religion has sold love, with the condition that you must be equal in God's sight to enter his domain. But love itself is more powerful than God, for love overcomes shadows, just as shadows cannot overcome the light. In love should be self-redemption. In love, you're overcoming your insatiable desire to do harm. So love itself is the image of utter perfection, not the perfection of being faultless, but the image of light.

Light is the overcoming of entropy. As Nietzsche so divinely tried to forget the fundamental aspects of human nature, affection is the connection to the universal consciousness of oneness, not some degradation of value. To walk away from love is to walk away from the consciousness of who you are. Love is the possession of light. It's not the possession of the body, it's the possession of the heart; two hearts made for the light, as it was always supposed to be for.

Love is the attachment of light. It's not the attachment of darkness, but it's the attachment of the soul connected to the consciousness of who you're. Two beacons created to discover the meaning of their lives through the senses of beautiful poetry. When I hear that love should not be attached, I say no, that's incorrect; you should be attached to your consciousness of who you are, your light of who you are, and your joy of what you are.Love is the most peculiar fire.

Love is commitment. Love is a weirdly exquisite expression of two hearts bound by an unequivocal firmament of hope and bewilderment. Love is unknowable at times; it's incredulous, it's credulous, it's respected by the illuminating functions of the decaying heart. Love is not only a beautiful thing, but it can only be seen by the senses. Only in the senses can love be found. It cannot be found by language. Poetry merely spears you; it merely shows you what love is like. But poetry encapsulates you with the clouds of the voluptuous sunsets of forever.

Love is an irregular and regular angle. It's like a formless tear on the brow of your lover. It's enchantment, it's the spirit, it's holy. It's courageous. It's truthful. Love is a galaxy in the brain where you kiss your lover forever. Love is the multiverse within all human minds. That's why love has limitless possibilities. Love is a poem rendered inside your brain cells. That's why your mood changes when you're in love. The poem changes from melancholic to a beautiful dolor made from the fragrances of Aphrodite's bejewelled arms.

WAYWARD

I stared out at the ghastly, and unpeopled streets and it was pouring and the smell of chaos entrenched me. The next moment, I saw a scarlet raven crow and I thought for moment it was Edgar Alan Poe trying to save me from myself, but it was nevermore.

I was sad, and dazed this loneliness consumed me, and Brooklyn felt infinitesimal the world was fading and my dreams were coming true that I was a raven evaporating into the deep blue foggy skies.

I was lost, and I did not want to be found I wanted some whiskey to dilute reality, nonetheless there is a sweetness in seeing the rain destroy everything.

OTHER STORIES IN NEW YORK

I gave up my power in the pursuit of truth. It is a very human thing to do that, to give up your own will for the needs of the many and not the few. Out of desperation, I hoped the bluebirds would appear to me in a dream to give me hope. I gave up security to attain insecurity because life mandated that by taking away everything I dearly held.

Movement is the catalyst of pain; life is simply unordered and dysfunctionally beautiful, like a hard-to-find book. There was unexpectedness everywhere when the rain fell potently. I felt that in my coat pockets I disliked change; change is a wasteland that doesn't nourish the soul. Having no one and having no friends was the best religion life could offer because there was no unreliability to my life. My pathways were guided by the badge and the typewriter. People were indecent, unreliable, and profusely unaware of their negative behavior. And in the end, what is left is nothingness. They provided me with nothingness. There is no guarantee of a return of the attention I gave to them.

I felt genuine contempt for people. I had anger raging inside my flesh. I don't know. I just felt helplessly contemptuous. I hated leaving the house when I lost her. I could see through people. It was straightforward how they communicated their contempt towards me by constantly patronising me. I trusted people. My trust was misplaced. What a waste of emotion on a sordid bunch of assholes. I give so much energy to things that reciprocate nothing to me. I felt that I didn't belong to the world, I belonged to her and her love. And in return, I would forget the world and make sure my cat was loved more than anyone else.

The people who murder for pleasure are missing something; a broken record, if you will. In New York seemed that way to me. I'd wake up in the morning, put on my dressing gown, go downstairs to boil the kettle, and find something was missing. A part of me was missing somewhere in all those gunfights. I lost a part of myself. NY makes you hooked on to the wrong kinds of things. Late night strip clubs visit pissing in Madison Square at 4AM. Mint moments of solidarity with men addicted to life's madness and deviance in general.

Suppose a man could drink a quarter rum every morning before work. Suppose he could make it from 9-5 without a care in the world. He'd have the world at his feet as opposed to the man who walked into the office contrite with a lemon tie bulging in the silhouetted sun from the windowpane of some obscure office window on Wall Street. For whatever reason, NY makes you hooked. NY is a jungle, and the best jungle on the planet. You wake up, go shave, and spend the rest of your day fighting for your freedom.

The sun in Sante Fe was blooded with a brilliance any man would hope to see. My apartment's bathroom tiles were weathered and old; they were mostly pre-WW2 gold with silver diamonds on the side.I thought that there was no better place to be. There was no better place to be than Sante Fe, and there were a few whores that were cheap I could demean myself with.

They'd see my silver revolver and my Remington typewriter and they'd want to fall for me straight away. They could not resist my terrible poetry. I heard Coltrane play on the radio at six and I was ready to make my rounds in the bars to find out who could have stolen that scarlet blue purse. Of course, of all the cases I had to be on, it would be that I had to travel from the Bronx all the way to California because she loved this purse and it was a late gift from her deceased husband. I would have to fund the journey myself. She was an aristocrat, but she wouldn't give me compensation until I brought the goods. I will bring the goods. The brusque smell of tenderising sweet steak bounced from the air outside my window in the upper-storey of this cheap hotel I was staying at. The noise of traffic, eloquently mixed in with the voided silence, intending to dominate my soul,

I ascertained the meaning of Manhattan: a wild jungle asleep; apportioned with the brilliance of the haphazard fog that crept dangerously under my hotel room door. Sore from the trip to Brooklyn, I slept in grandeur with Faulkner novels I stole from the Congress Library of NY all over the floor. I found beauty in this chaotic place. I found closure in the jungle of slaves who got up at 7:30 for work. I found eloquence in that rise. "Wake me up under the Tuscan sun," she said melodramatically. I thought that I'd very much like to hear her voice focused on the beauty and nakedness of my being. Wake me up under the sun in Tuscany, she said again drowsily and soundlessly, like a ship set to sail on calm seas in the Indian Ocean.

I thought if I woke her up she'd be angry and aimless as usual. I took a piece of bath salt made in Albuquerque. It was lavender. It was smooth and addictive, just how I liked it. Again, she said, wake up under the Tuscan sun. She was drowsy again, dreaming again of sifting darkness and spectral horrors. I couldn't implode on her sleep; all I could do was draw myself a bath, and watch the sun go down into the wastebasket of the void that is life; the passing mess of silent fog waltzed on the windowpane of the hotel suite; she was asleep as usual, emotionally incontinent, mellowly breathing slowly, but I was here for her in her dreamworld, and in this world I'll always be with her holding her hand into the passing darkness of the Tuscan sun.

JACOB

Fables of golden hair
tables of blackwood
flair, and the shorelines
of Sandy Bay alight with
a fever of the unknown
a sanctimonious strangeness
sweetness sweeps me of my
knees like Jacob returning home
a prodigal son given to God
given to an air hymn of clay
we will reborn with the third
rib made in hermetic rivers of
night, and I welcome this bounty
of allure a lavender poltergeist
of sensuous rubies I will cave
into your delight as this warms
my bones alright return your
love tonight

NEXUS

and to think
of silence
is to think of
your footprints
smashing
the sands with
electricity
a nexus of serenity
and I am engaged
to your method of
making the woods
smell like pepper
lilacs
and I am entrapped
in Isaiah's last
testament your eyes
lost in Malta.

HOWL

It felt like I was some insipid concoction, I wanted danger I dreamt of a dead body coming to shore. I wanted to be involved in mystery, the screeching, unforgivable, howling wind seemed to me to be a weird premeditated design it was if my troubling, and acute faculty of feeling was a game to the universe.

I decidedly devoted my time to taking the path of Walden I wanted the marrow of literature, yet the bruising wind oscillated a different story in mind: a story of characterological development of seeing through the periscope of plot, and the rot of the abyss. This whisper that pebbled towards me like a spectre on mescaline.

HEAVEN'S DOOR

I sit there at your hospital bedside table. You are drawing your last breath.
I am alone in this cruel, maddening world. What did I do to get here?
All my life is a collection of cruel events, one thing after another. I had
faith in God. I thought God was going to save you. Then again, I was
fantasising. My tears roll down the side of my cheek. I am lost, drowning
in self-pity. I know you did not wish this upon yourself, nor do you
wish the pain of the grief that is clearly upon me. When I think back to
the times in my childhood when you saved me from a life of absolute
torment,

Nobody wishes to sit here idly, powerless to do anything. I know in
your heart of hearts you wish to be healthy. Everybody wishes to be
healthy. I wish you to draw your last breath with joy in your mind. A
joy of a pain-free world. A world without cruelty. You surely lived a great
life, abundant with joy and faith. You took care of children with utter
unconditional love. There will be no one else like you. Human beings are
commonly selfish, but you, you were utterly kind. You were kind when
other people didn't deserve it. Your kindness was original; it was fresh,
and painstakingly brilliant. You could bring joy to other people's lives.
That was incredible. That was courageous. It was godlike.

As I sit here pondering your last breath, And the kind of life you endowed
me with. I get a sense of nostalgia. The Buddhists believe in
reincarnation. Well, ten years later, I see reminders of you everywhere.
Whenever someone else acts unconditionally, I believe that somehow
your essence is within them. I believe when I pass a stranger, opening the

door for me, that respect is alive. It is weird how so many things remind me of you.

From the grocery market, when people are truly kind and selfless when they allow you to go ahead of them to checkout, I feel that you are alive. I do not know what supernatural being conjured up this scenario, but it was kind of godlike. And you were godlike. Your nature was incredible. You were decisive and forthright. You were all that is good. I am saying "good" in the present tense because goodness as a natural quality is hard to come by. Perhaps you were born to be God. You acted in a way that represented what was possible for human beings.

PARIS CAFE

You look at me with fresh verbal ecstasy, enthralled by the chance of a happenstance.
You remark to your friend how grotesquely pure the rainstorm is outside in the first few chapters of Wuthering Heights.

You shape the atmosphere, sweet, delicate, and mellifluous, like seeing Pearl Jam live for the first time. I can't negate the fact that you are what I desire, yet any attempt at conversation is a risk. I could blow this like some guy in a romantic comedy.

I have often thought about how lovers meet in cafes on rainy days, and how the first meeting of attraction occurs in a storm of discontent.
There is a fire unheard of here; the thrust and thirst of love are uncoverable; if we both take a step towards the light, who will make it, me or you?

I heard a young group of academics next to me arguing about whether God is dead, and how the universe is cessation each moment at a time, but I was only interested in that young woman's long sylphlike legs; they were more distinguishable, charming, and real than the façade of God and the death of the universe. I mean, who cares? All I cared about was whether the taste of her lips was as smooth as the cappuccino I was drinking.

GREY SPARROW

All those grey sparrows
don't know the length and
the depths of your beautiful mania
I am the only creature of the Night
like Dracula naked piercing
hollow clouds and you are there
my friend a cello defacing
the willows in the moonlit shine
with a laugh your saving grace
causes me to fall to my knees
Don't you want to know how jesus
turned our night turned
our blight into sun tide
like an echo of something
left in death

MARY JESUS

Mary Jesus! poetry seems
better than words are worth
have you seen the change in me
a fire growing for your mirth
have you been dancing lately?
have you been remembering me?
have you cursed God & sought love
have you seen the arm's dove
how righteous are we?
you are trying to pretty me
like turtle doves on fire I can
feel what you need, and where
you bleed I see my lady being
freed by my creed I'm gonna give
you something more than a dead
deed

heaven's greatest love turning
bodies into what you sought
to see lit amongst those
stars I'm held by your bliss
euphoria on skin let the rain
drain away our pleas heaven
open thee, and humble us
angel oh Mary Jesus come to
see; and believe the oceans above
In Bob Dylan we trust

CULLODEN

The road to Culloden was a tapestry of shadow, and our horses galloped for days on end and the swift sharpening nightfall toned our skin with stories of Culloden and the specter of warfare. The sounds of swords smashing, and a myriad of men taking their last stand against the English. The weeping rhapsodies of blood filled the mud, and history was written. And the story was to be beautified for generations to come. Men of stature would write went on, and the stories were never the actuality, and they never knew of the men who died, and their hearts drunk on madness on rye, rum, and life. The cursed trail of blood, and the wind that shall never come again, the rains, the drums of sweat, and the lighting of flesh. Riveting, and pure the stories of old they shall never be told.

GEORGE

George stop walking around the house naked there could be a bomb going off any moment darling get into bed now you twit! Organise yourself for tomorrow's work. No Amy, I love walking around the house eating cheddar cheese on crisp burnt toast. Do not tell me what to do! What if the neighbours saw you all unclothed. I do not care said George with a heavy voice.

I like doing what I want to do. If I can enjoy a coffee and some marmalade on toast with cheddar cheese I shall have completed my life. You know life is short, and all, short and sweet like trousers dipped in lavender. I do not want to be remembered darling, if the Russians drop a bomb so be it.

Get to bed now George or else I am not cooking you breakfast tomorrow, and you will not have your favourite Colombian coffee with bacon burnt on toast with eggs on the side poached. You are completely irresponsible completely, I have never met a man with as much shamelessness as you. Get off your high horse dear, I can do what I want to do.

Let Hitler be raised from the dead, and let them march on me, but I tell you dear I shall enjoy this casual stroll down my hallway after all it is my house, and until I am dead nobody is going to stop me walking nakedly around this abode.

I tell you what a man has one life, and he deserves to walk nakedly in his own house. It's not like I am publicly exposing myself if you don't like it, dear go put on a virtual reality headset.

MAPLE

Maple syrupy skies
your blue
chestnut tears help me
climb my greatest fear
and we are sleepwalking
into the divine let's not lose
our touch your blueberry scent
is stamped all over my shoulders
do you remember that
labyrinthine note of love stuck
to my footprints on Long Beach
the echo of Plutarch is
in our eyes this winter night.

MEADOW

Tribulated by the sheer storm growing outside Meadow starkly looked and looked for a skylark dancing on a limb. Meadow bided her time as the storm was rolling in remarkably. How smooth, and brilliant it was to see the raindrops hit the earth, relaxed, and unafraid she guzzled down her Italian espresso.

The windowsill was a bright blood veined red sullied and painted nicely. Meadow knew that time was unfriendly, and that it got the best of her. She'd happily fall asleep reading the latest thriller.

To Meadow nothing else mattered, but this gaze at the rain it took her whole soul to look away for the rain was her otherworldly adventure, she imagined herself dancing on clouds, and singing some song in French. And she would stretch her godly arms scintillatingly with the freshest courage to overcome the world dancing in the rain is the easiest thing you could ever do.

CAB POEM

Slowly I think of
mountain streams
and ash rivers combustible
and song worthy of your praise
tenebrous silhouettes of forgotten
pine trees and birch forests
all waltzing and
crisp a siberian cat
gazes me and I fall
into an abyss of
neon purrs

HUSH

Hush lovely we are dreaming of rugged cliffs battered and bruised, and caked by the merciless cold of the ocean, your hair blowing in the wind on the foot of the cliff. Your legs cold, warm, elegant, shaped by melody shaped by fading mist. You needn't muster any courage, or strength for there is nothing to gain but to be swept away with the storm.

Take your thoughts and jump into that storm jump in and drown in beauty in wickedness in solace in silence in a dance of sheer nature. Remember all those times drinking bourbon under those pine trees the stinging stormy lush beauty of being alive of being wild of being disquieted of being roughened by the end of all things.

Jump not later, but now let the music swallow and slaughter all that you are and when the music is done with you let your last breath be the sea.

THE HIGH WINDOW

Annie stared into the spiralled multifaceted window and thought what could have been. She thought what life could have been like if she was a rose coming to life in spring, and she thought what it would've been like to be the noontide, and she felt sudden asphyxiation in her heartstrings. There was a melody to gazing into the past. It was surreal to think about what could have been, and it was easy to lose yourself in the lucidity of the moment.

We don't get to choose our story The multifaceted window of life chooses the story for us, and that story could be a tale of sacrifice or a tale of love that conquers death and life itself. Annie thought more and felt drawn to the conclusion that simplicity is not the key to life; the key to life is to stay in character and to face whatever may come head-on.

As Annie's breathed slowly, her purple moon lips escaped reality. She was compelled to place her hands on the mirror to proclaim to life that she wasn't going to be lost in the facade of memory, she was going to dance and dance well beyond fear, beyond judgment, beyond the noise of the crowd.

The mirror spoke to Annie and said, "Do not choose death, choose life in every moment. Don't live abruptly, live not in avoidance of the truth, live despite suffering, live in spite of death, live in spite of pain, choose the story of love to forget the past's wind. If you do, it'll rupture you. For we are born to live in the moment, and that's all we can do. "

PORTRAIT

The throbbing mountain mist squeezes your skin affectionately. You are only looking at a portrait of a mountain. You are stateless, and the timeless oak trees relieve you. You are not impressed by the noise and racket of the city, and you have a bottle of tequila in your hands.

You don't want to leave your apartment; it is filled with Murakami and plenty of records by Beethoven. Why leave the apartment? You have enough silence contained in your walls that it smooths your anxiety.

You want to stretch your arms beyond the realms of Europe. You want to see the sea birth the king tides, and you want to see the silence of the moonlight jading and hitting the water. You want to leave your footprints on the beaches of Bondi. And you want to leave a letter for me to find? You want to, and you aspire to be an ardent lover like Elizabeth Lavenza. You want to disappear and become enveloped in the verse of Emily Dickinson. You want to escape. You already have since you are my dream.

AWAKENING

I sat in my red checked flannel shirt, sipping whisky and admiring the sunset. I was drowning my sorrows, drowning myself in fear of forgetting the past. I wanted the past to become a fog, but I couldn't exude any confidence to get myself out of this rut. Watching the stars pass by in memory, I felt the vaguest arm touch my shoulder, as if the ghost of myself had ventured far away. I swear by the good graces of God that I'd stop drinking, that I'd buy a girl some flowers, that I'd kiss a girl in the rain. But the death of my mother had come over me. The sweltering heat. It was so hot sitting here on Bondi Beach in the lonesomeness of the sunset. I remember the days of walking aimlessly, my feet leaving footprints, my heart sunk into the sands, my feet vanishing into the cold or hot sands. I see myself venturing off in a moment. But I love being lost in my mind.

I love being alone, and sometimes this aloneness inspires me to do more than just think. But, I think that we are all slaves to our past in some capacity. One way or another, death is going to come to us, whether it is the death of somebody else or the death of a loved one. Death takes many forms; the death of motivation is one.

The unwillingness to wake up, the unwillingness to follow our own dreams. But now I'm back in the prison of my own sins, and no one will ever know what I've gone through. I do pity myself. I pity those people who have love and throw it away. I pity those who have chances but squander them. "The mass of men lead life in quiet desperation," Henry David Thoreau said ever prophetically. I feel that to be ever more true; we are the victims of our ideals, and for that reason, I believe it is profitable to let go. Let go of it. Become more than your ideals; become free.

ITALO CALVINO

You left the finest
kiss on my thighs
and I shared your flesh
incorporeal and true
remember my blood on
that marble table those
nights of forgetting cain
and abel and babel
feels so close the zenith
of our predicaments will
be over and you are the
apparition I don't want to
lose that swift hosanna
I want to hear that prayer
of raindrops and violets
of nights where Italo Calvino's
city is our love drenched in
the honey growing in Nice

WHITE CRIMES

To whom the night falls
and the shrieking mind of
lost pebbles of lines and sorrow
be it a displaced melody, a second
 entity, and of love of
the grace of hinterlands in space
you speak to me through the rubble
of my ancestry in the dream time
a koala whispers the lost tales
of my kind their souls splintered
by white crimes.

NEW ORLEANS

They were having a
fiesta next door fucking
  saying God's name
in vain I watched
the dust settled on my bookshelf
Gertrude Stein it was tonight
four cigars, and an uncommon
appetite for boredness
I watched the sin of the city pass
and I thought of going to
New York, but I didn't have
the finance, still I thought of
New York bookstores
filled with first editions of
Women by Bukowski
I watched homeless people
beg for their food
and a priest walked past and
didn't say a thing
I smoked four cigars and
the downpour
made everyone go home
the centre of Hobart felt
like a vacant New Orleans
car park it was
beautiful to see
at last

WHITEWASHING

The sprawling shadows accompanied us. We foraged the dark loneliness of creation, incinerating, eschewing the deep ridge and divide of human potential, with bloodstained memoirs in our pockets.

Burning fetuses, marrow, and cold sparrows. Flocked on the ground aflame, the white folks implemented their culture's slaughter fastidiously with no integrating spirit. Their minds were filled with rivers of gold and thoughts of Sydney being theirs. They didn't know their minds were rivers of hegemonic trash. A culture perpetuating a destructive force will be riveting for centuries to come.

White folks think civility is bringing them their privilege. They think civility is poisoning waterholes. They think civility is the introduction of unnaturalized animals.

They think civility is bringing their church choirs and vehement doctrines to an end because the aboriginal people's religions are not good enough. They think civility is tearing families apart. They think civility is cognitive dissonance. They think civility is bringing sugar and telescopes, but they bring no love, but the destruction of an entire people. Mankind has made mistakes, but true civility can be taught only by togetherness, not by control.

MELBOURNE MOONBEAMS

The moonlight intensely pounced off your elegant cheeks. You seemed unaware of my presence. Your legs were crossed and you seemed to have no care in the world. Reading Freud like a maestro, the jazz music swayed your breasts uncaringly. And I felt the need to come over to you. The ambience of the Burlesque club in Melbourne was intensely gratifying because you were there.

I can remember that dress you wore. A pickled red dress, a black luxor coat, a Russian soviet union beanie, and a renegade woman. You were a free thinker. Oh, I wish I had met you in a bookstore. We could have all the kinds of conversations intelligent individuals would have. We would talk about life, existentialism, and the process of death and what motivates us to keep on going. I thought that you were a godsend and that you reading Freud was a sign like me finding the Search for Meaning by Viktor Frankl in the bushes in Hyde Park. I had a penchant for loving a woman who loved books and cats more than humanity. I thought that kind of woman was a rare occurrence in nature.

The jazz music keeps on playing. I felt starless, but I had to talk to you. The intensity is far too high. The timber floor is godlike when your feet touch it. Maybe you will like me. Maybe you will kiss me like a woman in danger. Maybe you will love me. Who knows, maybe we will dance to Sinatra in the street when it rains, and we will both wear trench coats when the frost sullies all the dahlias. I feel like buying you a diamond, baking you waffles engrossed in cheese, and we should drink rye when the sun comes up after frisky bodies touching to the sound of Count Basie. I wonder what you are thinking of me since you are staring at me with a hummingbird smile that is sincere, warm, and honest. I want to say my thoughts on the patriarchy to you. I would love to be dominated by you. I want my world to be dominated by you. I hope you love that. I believe women should have equal power. I hope that you love expressos and french toast with blueberries wrapped in honey because that's what I am reading from your vibes. Your petite brown hair, your curly lips, silhouetted by a mystery. I am trying to understand. I never want the jazz to stop playing. I don't want this moment to end. I don't want this to end. I will eternalise it in Sylvia Plath's jar of poetry.

BABY BOB DYLAN

And when love first
touched my hands
I felt like a baby
Bob Dylan
sweetly aligned
with the blues
and the sun drew
me close
I once attempted to
run away from my
home, thinking my
mother wouldn't know
she called the cops, and
I was hiding out the back
and she told me, son
I love you so
don't ever go
don't ever go
 I love you so.

WOMAN

the men who have merit denounce
their angst towards female influence
as the nature of patriarchy is to denounce
female authority in this new war on truth
we have arisen from the ashes becoming a
force to be reckoned with, masculinity
should be about the giving up of egos
diversity mens to share the sparse
indifference towards each other however
brutal it is, we must love.

THINKING BACK

seven years ago
I was poor lonely and broke
fat, undesirable,
unemployed
I watched sun
wash me away
I knew there were
poems in me and
I would think about
odes in the shower
thinking one day
I might have
a cat to call my own
a lady to smother me
with kisses of appreciation
of no sombreness only
the glorification of love
which Anne Sexton talked
about, I kept on going
now I am filled with the
journey of the blues
making me better than
true.

NOBODY

nobody
wants to
understand
misery like
me
I am unshaped
a back porch of
trilliums chewed up
by an album of
deep grace
I can't save face
only this back porch
knows where I have been.

POISON BE

poison be
the chatter
of the crowd
my weirdness
prefers nuance
my weirdness
might be wry
and it might be
dry to you
at least it has
heart at least
it bleeds
a crimson
nightingale
talking of John
Keat's name.
romanticising
only rainy days
only rainy days.

MUSING

I wait for inspired musings
to show up to my front
door, Bukowski
says to me live a little
but don't live by my
shadow, live by yours
and I think of how he
talked about Celine
and I wonder
what Bucharest is like
at night is it better
than delight?

DEAD LEAVES

 I see a tabby
rolling in the dead leaves
of Autumn and
I think
what a life
it must be to be so
comfortable with time
and there is an atonement
of biblical proportion in
the way a cat views the world
if only I can have that answer
yet maybe it is wonder.

WINTERISE

someone says to me
what do you do
in your spare time?
I am trying to find
grace through
the tearing of sinew
I am finding viscerality
I am finding Persephone
I am finding the truth
of seasons
I winterise myself
with the maxims
of Nabokov

A LOT

It takes a lot
to write about your
soul and feel to
unknown
it takes a lot
for you to touch
heaven with
an unfeeling hand
it takes a lot
open up your heart
and see where it rots
and to see where
you can withstand
the unbearable
pain of existing
it takes a lot
to face the emptiness
it takes a lot
to save yourself
today
take love
and leave it open
you deserve to win
again you deserve
to see you bloom

to see hell doomed
for real, but it takes
a lot to be you.

SONGED

don't let the tides
of opinion
change the way
you love yourself
don't let it drown your
innocence
don't let them take
you, you of daffodils
and pure sea tides
glowing
songfully.

KUNANYI

the gentleness
of the mist
mystified
our passion
for the weary
Kunanyi mountain's
pathos
forced
rethink
the art of
breathing

MY TOXIC MASCULINITY

A great portion of the population believes that attraction, and shared interests are reasons to be with somebody that a spark is necessary for love to frequent your own body. I beg to differ, I think that idea complicates things other people believe that you must experience butterflies to understand love. I experienced that stimulation many years ago. As men our society teaches us to appear invulnerable, and any emergence of emotion is a sign of being candid and weak. Perhaps that is a facet of an ever-growing conundrum of how mankind perceives love. Making the woman washing the dishes is a sign of strength the woman must be dependent on the man for social security. These behaviours or as Carl Jung the famous psychiatrist's idea that conscious is a multifaceted problem we all have archetypes we all have our own mythos to deal with (the story we tell ourselves) growing up I was taught that courtship was about making sure that the woman was loved, and not threatened.

I used to take Lovan because my depression was immense, I was suicidal, and extremely desperate. Nothing worked I tried everything to cure my depression. My life was in ruination for awhile i had to move states, coming to somewhere completely unknown and that made completely vulnerable. I was alone, I didn't have many friends. And, I didn't know how to figure out things for myself. I dropped out of university a few times because of frequent bouts of depression, and anxiety I started smoking, and drinking regularly because nothing eased my anxiety. Drinking, and smoking exacerbated my intrusive thoughts. Honestly, I didn't know how to express myself properly until, I started writing poetry. I read a few novels by Charles Bukowski, and I related to him a lot, and through days of commitment to writing my feelings out on paper, I begun to understand the root of my problems. My problem was that I always repressed my emotions, I didn't express them. And this is a common problem for a lot of young men.

Bukowski taught me to keep on going when everything felt like nothingness. Poetry aligned the

My father taught me that the woman should have equal dependence as the male would. Holding back emotions was a sign of weakness. Attraction is merely a magnet, love is the essence that glues things together as a writer one of the greatest things, I love about my woman is that she does not like my writing. She is the one person who does not have any interest in my art, and to me that is brilliant because I use my art as a façade to express what cannot be expressed by actions. In my late fifteens I dated many women well obviously because my puberty permitted me to. I never knew solitude then I was aroused by the moment electricity by exploring things, I had never done before like kissing a woman that was alien to me.

I guess I learnt what, I knew about female behaviour from jerks, and misfits who thought that being a jerk was the way to go about when in interaction with a woman. I however did not behave in that way. Romanticism is and was an important part of my development especially Shakespeare, I got a better understanding about women when, I read Shakespeare and Oliver Twist which was an utterly profound story about hardship, and how love always endures the ficklest of fortunes that a person can face. Perhaps that is the answer to toxic masculinity we need to really rethink how we court women chivalry should be relevant, but women should be respected for how self-reliant they are. Men to see woman as equals because being in opposition never has really helped the ongoing feminist movement is result of that factor. We have to view these relationships we share in terms of how society operates we have to direct these people to a new level of relationship.

Each relationship we share with each other is a sum of all the other relationships that are in the world. In other words, the change to how women are treated at home because the real changes start at home when you think that your spouse, or partner should do more work than you because you work more hours than you have to get off your high horse, I don't want to come off as too preachy but that's where the change happens when you are willing to put your needs aside to compromise on key things that directly affect how you feel about each other those unwashed dishes could change the world if you would only get in. It is essential men become role models for other men especially how men write about women especially on social media. Men are living in its a not my problem culture they will blame the way the treat women on their childhoods but that's the problem. It's the fact men have problems with women being equally smart. This competition has to end. I had this competition going on in my mind for so long, I had to strive to be better than other men because other men where trying to outperform me in my efforts at gaining a woman. But perhaps I was gaining the wrong attention perhaps I was gaining something, I didn't need. And that was true in my entire efforts through out my entire teenage life I strived to gain attention from women and it never helped me internally. I questioned my own confidence continously, and those behaviors had an expiration it was by not searching. stars for me. Don't give up on your passion it can find what you need.I found the woman of my dreams because poetry begged me not to give up. And she really is a poem to me.I didn't think my poetry would become human, but I am glad that the universe aligned us to be together. I am glad for her, and poetry, & my cat.

Male writers should advocate for these changes we need men talking about rape, and how our culture has become totally misguided on the treatment of women for thousands of years women have been belitted, and oppressed. Men to stop and think for one moment how they should treat women on tinder, or facebook on any medium they communicate with women, the old phrase goes without saying, would I like to be treated this way. And in their minds they would directly say no. I would not we have to say to ourselves that women are equal it needs to become an affirmation because until we acknowledge this problem at the core that we are driven by control, we will always be in opposition to one another. As expressed before a part of the problem is the power dynamic structure the ongoing power for control, when an unbalance occurs within the set structures of a relationship there is a chance that both people are not getting recipcrocation. My toxic masculinity began this way because, I had these reoccuring insecurities because I didn't have a job. I felt needy, unhinged, aghast, angst, it was like I did not have any direction, I had to have stability.

I had to have a job because that is the modern day occupation of the man, or the standard belief shared by a many people. A man's income is the measure of his purpose it was up to the man to provide for the woman, however, my view has changed. I think if you are in love it is up to you to make that relationship and your income is not the factor in deciding whether or not you are successful in love. By changing my thoughts on dependence in terms of relying on a woman for various things, I began to feel better this growing insecurity went away; my existence was not going to decided on procreation, or the size of my wallet. By changing the way I felt about doing everyday household jobs after my 9-5 job helped me. I saw that doing my woman's laundry as a good thing, and not a bad thing, although some days I hate doing it as most people do after they work all the day only to come home and cook dinner for their partners. It is up to us to group together in solidarity to achieve the same goal, and to be go about these changes in a disciplined manner that ironing your woman's clothes is not a bad thing it is actually is a powerful act of equality because you care enough for you will not make this about you. We have to say it is powerful, charming to cook a woman's meal day in and day out if the woman has a busy workload. It is up us to be reliable, and hardworking men by working on how our woman feels after work if we work on this you will see considerable changes it happened to me.

My existence towards women is measured merely by how, I love them, and how I treat them equitably. Us men like to feel superior it is hardwired into our biologies, but we do get to decide how we treat each other. This is where the new evolution begins new rules must come into play especially for male writers we are responsible for the advancement of how women are treated we are responsible for influencing, and dividing people whether that be through the academic, political institutions that make up our societies as a whole. Thus a new rule be written an ethical standard that has to be adopted by all men that it is our obligation to help women feel secure.

THYME

Here I am
cutting and taking
in the thyme and it is
tumultuous and
windy outside
and I think of that
one night in Berlin
your hair rubbing
against my neck
you drink tequila in one
hand and forget
time again and I
kiss your earlobes
here I'm cutting
onions thinking
of time again
thinking of loving
you again.

LOSE MYSELF

And dreamless I'm
sometimes I understand
why Virginia Woolf drowned
her sorrowful heart hounded
by hell, and I understand why
Sylvia Plath lost her soul to
Ted Hughes, and understand
it's hard being alone
without grace, don't romanticise this
melody, it's folly to try and
be jolly and I'd rather
watch the sun crawl down and
the clouds die down then to
get lost in a crowd.

SEASICK

Sick boned was the sky
amusing with no
fright and I of no delight
seasick
near a shore barren
weightless
musicless
muscleless
and as the moonbeams
caked the ole oceanfront store
of a takeaway store
I was inundated with Chopin's
allegro maestoso
with a windless
torment I want freshness
and a viper Juliet.
succumbing to the
tides and thrust my neck
into the blues awaiting
you awaiting a miracle
a feeling
which you stole me from
inside

I FOUND BROOKLYN

I harbored no judgment for the stupid, or disdainful. I kept to myself, busying myself with perusing old, and out of print books. Reality itself was troublesome, and frankly something I tried to avoid at all costs. I wore a mask socially speaking. I didn't have time for people or conversation in general. I loved the disquiet moments of staring into nothingness at nighttime, I loved walking alone in the rain. I felt godless but quite content with the beautiful starkness of my solitude. The lonesome winters in Brooklyn were tragically attractive, there was a kind of quiet in reading books alone at Central station. I enjoyed thoroughly reading Faulkner, Nabokov, and Charles Dickens. I was the unlikeliest winner in the battle for love. Seldom did I think of wanting to be with someone. But one day, I felt a lovebird emerging out of the abyss. She was the kindest love I had ever met. She was the epitome of genius the craftiest lover.

She walked into me whilst I was waiting for a train. She had that, a glare that soul-crushing affectionate, mind one that knew what poetry you needed. Not only did she know what music I liked, she knew who I was without even meeting me. She held me in the moonlight, she eyed my vulnerabilities and was gentle-spirited, and softhearted. Oh, she was Brooklyn. She was the novel I frequented too often. For I read about her in a novel once and the same plot Point happened to me; her beauty slaughtered me.

The midsummer dream of her velvety silver dress glowed and gnawed at my mind incessantly. To dream of such beauty and such kindness is otherworldly. The anticipation, and the music that swept my mind in a tour de force of truth, revealed to be a constant truth. That beauty is a fleeting song, a rapturing song that engages the entirety of one's being. Though I had been living alone for a while and the screech and bustling business of reality unsettled me. I continued to dream; contented with the spectred light that danced my eyelids to sleep, I was caught by the entrapment of sirens that soothed the anxieties of my soul.

Such is the timeless gospel of being human, the soaring fading light, and we always dare not to dream. We dare not to be bold, but if the dream world is the only place to feel truly alive, then one must dream boldly. Nonetheless, I felt my soul at ease when I came home from work. I decided that sleep is not the enemy of life, but sleep is the real hero.

For our days are obviously numbered, and we do not have the sufficient lifespan to waste our lives away idly. Sleep is the rapturing that we often need. When reality is insufficient, there is poetry to this relaxing easing, this uncomplicated dichotomy that sleeps and the dreamworld are two different worlds, and we are to become terribly beautiful when our eyes are closed.

There is an idyllic truth and evocative realisation when we find that our dreamworlds are in fact the fabric of who we are. A wavelength to vitalise our beings. What are we without our dreams? Vessels of nothingness kindling nonexistence. But our dreams course truth throughout the marrow of who we are.

Aren't you beautiful? the lilacs call you by name, and the sun has inundated you with the prettiest soul of all. You are akin to the pleasurable beauty of Thetis. You dance and walk on the water gracefully. You are the heroine of all women, your profundity as gorgeous as the poetic marvel of The Hesperides.

You are prophetic, musically godlike, your dress is silky dactylic pentameter. I have heard of your sea-grown soul a thousand miles away. Your dream lives on inside of me. I am awestruck by the passage of time you hold in your mind the serenity of our sunlight. There is nothing more purposeful than this message, this serendipitous melodic feeling. I venerate your skin and I disremember the world, but I hold on to you. For you are etched into my very eyes, your essence is singing within me. Your mountainous hair and your incalculable intelligence soothe me. You smell like English Oak, soothingly scintillating. And I began to wonder how your prodigious soul walked into my life. I know you are mirthful and deathlessly joyful. I have seen you and thought of you. When I walk near evermore flowing rivulets, your joy dances into me. And I see the world as it should be, not as I'd like it to be.

CELLO STAND

I
Standing on a cello
in front of a moonless
ocean you void
and enter the wellspring
of hell circumcised in mind/
what is more arrogant

II
complicit in madness
they stand yet you
of love and of trauma
stand on that cello
inflame devoted
to an opening beyond
the mundane.

III
For there is no
deeper feeling than
the sanctum than love
the sanctum of
words not held.

WEEPING CAT

Enclosed is the
autumnal weight
of your miserable
shadow, secluded and
impassioned you are
idled in a room of
fresh magnolias
perfumed with regret
your form is vintage
sweetness a Bulgarian
sun shower here I
remember the air
in which we sought out
our grievances, where the
deciduous leaves fell
onto the cat that weeps.

HELSINKI

A profound
strangeness coats
our necks
where the skies
vacate our emotion
strung in vivid commotion
swept before our knees
I in you, a paradise
that peels away
our recollection
of Helsinki
mudded in the unbeknownst
tapestry of Isaiah's empathy
for a verse
of a verse in droplets of
repetition,
 I would love to add a feeling
to this lyric
yet you stop my heart
from beginning
I do not understand
where this comes from
this self-conscious urge
to drape the world with
my mirth, a joy
of you in joy
in melody attached

to the expanse of starlight
a corridor into the realms
of mythic delight.

APPETITE

I have no appetite
for time I gaze at the sun
it does not feel new
I stare at the ground
I feel nothing
I see a juniper blooming
nothing feels the same
I have no appetite
for beauty
no appetite
for nature
no appetite
for colour no
appetite for
love.

DYSTOPIA

the darkness is verisimilitude
and the newspapers
are burning the press is
burning we are living
angst in a dystopia where
belligerence rules where
dreams are lost where
madness is common and
originality is uncommon
treachery is borne cynicism
 is the ruling principle it is
your choice is your voice
 that matters if you'd only
make it brighter.

MUTAWINTJI

We treasure those memories of the fleeting sun and the mirthful warmth of existence. Trout fishing was our escape, having a barbecue, and our warm summer evenings talking about how different shaped clouds were poetic and soul-relaxing. We took our swags all the way to Coober Pedy with our backpacks filled with novels and our compass. We wanted to live naturally, dangerously, with love. Miranda loved the openness of walking along the road all the way through the dust.

We bivouacked in Arnhem Land, travelled down to Broken Hill, and went to places like Mutawintji, where the great desolate caves gave us warmth. We travelled across oceans of darkness and red sand where the light met us first at the Flinders Ranges. Her Holden commodore had broken down, and I was working as an indigenous ranger.

I thought it was my job to help anyone that was bogged down. Well, I thought it was my moral virtue. These lands are crazy, and as you get further out of the bush, the dry really will unsettle anybody who isn't used to the land. As fresh as that memory was in my mind, it was her auburn hair and cheeky Australian grin that hooked me. She was deeply troubled, but she woke up a fire in me. She taught me more than the laws of the land; she taught me the laws of love. That uncertainty is the pillar of attraction.

ULURU AND MY STARS

The moonlit   Simpson Desert
 is a tumultuous
wave of broken corsets
of sun-like sand, the
trails go afar the
didgeridoo sonata is
 the Kangaroo man of the
 Olga's Uluru lies there asleep
  with all the deadly beautiful
  dreams of the dreaming
 a lifetime of ceremonial
dances are stuck to
insides of Uluru's caves like the
 lifelikeness of my people
I can see it rain on the
 rock I see the rainbow
 serpent waltzing with
 the droplets of heaven,
 I sit wide awake staring at
the Milky way from my tent,
my soil is the earth of this place,
 Australia my rock of
 glory my ancestors
were slaughtered by the
 white settlers, but our
poetry lives on inside the night sky

WAS

Cursed the pilgrimage was
abstract our destiny was
like a peanut tortured
by the melodic tension of being
we sought to parody the sunlight
like Hamlet on amphetamines
tense, and terse the passage
to victory is senseless and myopic
the tragedy was, and all of our
passions passed wondering
and dancing in corridors
of an abandoned asylum
cursed this sentence was
to be exiled in nonsense
a Kafkaesque Trial; an awkward
and strong avocado
crushed in an ominous fog.

TOM WAITS

Somebody is watching us
in the bushes a
gargoyle wearing red
velvet pants and we
yearn for soup from
Leonard Cohen a lyrical
snake, Tom Waits
for us in the dark
where the olive trees
reaches clouds like
Nick Cave's last
song, oh my
what a lasting song
we want in our arms
in our arms this
absurdity is the reason
we live beyond the dark.

LUSTFUL HORROR

Indescribable unfathomable
immeasurable is your psychedelic
ghostly gory blooded clothed body,
river of corpses, blood circling
the vortex of dark bats the well
filled with crepuscular cut off
arms and legs broken bones
a forest of mutilation dead bodies
everywhere hanging from trees
homicidal cottages, suicidal notes
draped in blood hanging from red
roses skulls beneath my feet
reapers and vampires, men impaled
on crucifixes dark robed men
scarred chests made of human organs,
it snowed blood and rained
blood every single day.
uncontrollable urges lissome
sensual energy superior than reason,
secluded cyclone sweat
and bones a lover's throne,
her breasts up against my body
I felt her smother me with an
incandescent frozen anorexic
bodies climbing up the muddy
slide to the top where they shall
get hanged again; each day the

rotting smell would be a symphony
we ate maggots out of the brains
of corpses, ravens fly gracefully
abundantly in the night, closets with
wolf manufactured wefts, we're
one erotic story
our sex burnt everything in sight,
blindfolded in a room no light you
and me feeling each her eyes
locking me up outside,
her lust met mine under the siren's forest,
a melancholy tale, the universe exploded
we destroyed all the planets and stars
cause we're the lust the lust of death,
we're the murderers of breath a
passionate rhyme more than
prurience more than indecorous
nights no one can stand against
our distasteful fight.

3 AM

I will get through this
the sun will live in
me when I'm asleep
at night, I will get through this
I will be alive again
I will be singing with Whitman
on the shoulders of dead Gods
I will let the light through in
the shadows of my wounds
at 3AM anything is possible
death or a goodnight
I will get through this
I keep repeating this to myself
with a cannula in my arm
with plenty of grace l shall be
I will get through this
I will be me I think
 of mountains capped
in golden river fog I think
of Glasgow at night
I will get through this tonight
I will find myself again
In this hospital moonlight
with Count Basie and Jack
Kerouac on my side and
Whitman in my sight I'll be
alright I keep thinking of

death and a goodnight
but I got love it's better
than this blight the man
next to me in the other bed
lost his sight, his crying keeps me
up I'll be alright I have love on my
side a lyrical refuge
of night at 3AM
in this hospital
I continue writing some lines
of grace

1:48 AM BUKOWSKI

Here I am 28
reading a bukowski
poem at 1.43 AM
in the morning before
my colonoscopy
not afraid
just turning back and
forth in bed
aches down my
thighs, redish cheeks
I didn't want to be alive
the ulcers and my lower
intestine are on fire
blood floods out of
.my anus uncomfortable
I'm on the toilet
reading a Bukowski poem
to get me through the pain
reading to let my tears smooth
into the drain
I think of how Hank walked
the streets of New Orleans
looking for a diner to eat in
and a place to watch
the horror show continue
the horror of seeing the rain
fade when all you want

223

for it is for it to continue
to glow and see the droplets
peak climb of the roofs
of abandoned apartments
and all the world continues
to fade in a way
that I want that pain to fade in
the nurse helps reput my cannula
in as it has gone astray
the dressing is dead
I'm waiting for
the muse to be dread.

NASCENT

There is a
nascent tulip within
writhing your every
essence
shortness of breath
lengthens your death
believe in love your
never regret
the middle of our
leafy melody fixed
in shadow and no
remorse
our paradise
that begins
our paradise
that begins

ARTIE SHAW

and if we don't do
art, what
fire do we have
to keep us
alive in misery
my friend? only
love knows the
length of this road
only loves glows
that story into the
moon rays of
Artie Shaw.

BROKEN GRACE

there is more
to this frost
than meets the eyes
there is rejuvenation
and a holier
ghost that yearns
to seep into our throats
here I am at the edge of rain bridge
with daggers in my thighs
coloured by your truthfulness
coloured by Australian Wattles
and your garlands are shadowless
and I accentuate broken grace
and you take the sap
if my being and make it
great, and maim my lost
story

CODDLE

as we coddle
each other's fire
I forget the reason
of despair
I forget the nature
of nature
I only remember
this closeness
of wind
and rain

STARRY NIGHTS

tempestuous
trust in
grottos
of wonder
and we ponder
the stillness of
Vincent Van Gogh's
Starry Nights
and we want to
know what
he knew

NURSE

and here I am
bleeding out
comforted by
the help of nurses
the help
of love.

HUMPBACK WHALE

and we
are told to
shove our pain
down and let the
world judge our
identities
I say be poetry
be a song of yourself
be a song Whitman
glistening stone
that rises you into
a hearth of moving
waters
beyond the greyness
of cessation
and blue
oceans with
rhyming bodies
of humpback whales

NIGHT WE MET

the night we met
jovial white
auburn roses
turned our hands
into clouds of
silence that sliced
all the those days
I was in the emergency
anxious lost
depraved of honest
joy depraved the song
that attached itself
to my weak
veins.

HELD

I don't want to
be held by anyone else
only your lips that rescind
time
and make
the morning glories glow
and I see it now
all those terrible
struggles
all those tears
dead and not alive
thrive my eyes
your vagabond
likeness
is the road
that needs
to never be forsaken

AUTUMN

what matters
is that you still
the glow
in Autumn
what matters is
that love
still affects
your bones
and tours
and exhales
the grace
that you
deserve.

LONG BEACH

I walked home jumping up and down
on the road looking for inspiration in
the tar of where the cars drove for
miles on end, then I realized Long Beach
was in my fingers for the forbidden sheets
of ice like sand followed me home to help me wash. away the lyrics of
our forbidden starry
Marimba night. The wilderness of love grew on our shoulders like Atlas
was our name so be it the
falling stars of the blue rue
we gathered out hearts and hungered
for the luminiferous auroras lights
that waltz with waters of Long Beach
it was unlit the florescent hues of the romantic
meadows of Long Beach, a severed
dawn, and a the simplistic moon collapsed on our
dreams, the immortality of the murky rocks
made us forget the times we had kissed
in Florence, as the tides of The River Derwent
were jubilantly unscarred, and scathingly
beautiful, I had found a mirror of time to
reflect in a vineyard stapled with our kisses
a mausoleum bearing no death but romantic
poetry seemed to be the recognition of

moments by Long-Beach holding hands
and seeing the luminosity of sorrow lit so
farce in the dunes of the cemetery of heartwarming
ecstasy.

GREEN SEA

And the exhausting length
of the mist in a sea salted
spur of oceanic
light swallowed the valley
near the estuary
and the design of the
minted Green algae near
the curvature of the sand collapsed
the melody in my mind
thinking of glacial shapes
and the clouds were formless
and they were as sparse
as the feelings in my head
they were just droplets
of passion of unknowable colour
and here I'm awake
finding something of worth
extracting song from uncertainty
extracting a reason to go on
finding something
to grow a diaphanous white lily
near our voices silence our worries
and this imagery will last beyond
this night.

WHEN THE SUN DOES NOT RISE
IN HOBART

A dreary night of caution the moonless reflection in my mirror and the anticipation that something was bound to happen out of the ordinary, yet most of the time I reflect on the thought that something is going to happen I go back to sleep. It was the 24th of June 2014, and I do not what I am doing with my life. My room was filled with books all the good sorts, Bukowski, Poe, Whitman, Nietzsche, all these drunkards that I never got to meet.

My bed was somewhat abusing my loneliness excessive my need to smoke incredible the wind in Hobart was cruelly beautiful the streets at night unpeopled and I stare out the window waiting for something, only the rushing of the wind against my chest made me very indifferent, I suppose I was indifferent would that change the world. Hobart you cold miserable beautiful sad disquieting place. You grow on me HOBART like your sharp wind that brushes, and rages against my skin. Hobart you venerable honourable worthless jewel of Australia with your mount Wellington, and your Antarctic winters. Your coldness is troubling you grimace me.

I was unemployed without purpose without ambition without colour without love without cats what was I going to do? Where was I going to go. The only thought that made its presence known in my head was sitting down and writing a bunch of poems. Poetry the sweetness of death exuded efficiently in a manner that was intoxicatingly brilliant poetry was hard to write it was harder than trying to commit suicide because all you had to was jump, and soon it was over poetry however was different it lingered like a dreadful sickness like something you could never fully recover from.

And here I was fat lazy, indolent, and lacking ambition and I all I could think was about the sweetness of somebody's else lips I could taste their intelligence with every drop of word I poured out, I assumed my identity was sitting here idled away from the displeasures of being human. Yet I wanted to be a poem I wanted to be on the paper, I wanted to be disconnected from the animality of being human.

It was here in the empty wine-bottles, and the unread books that I found the nature was in assuming who you wanted to be. I did not know how I was going to write a book let alone survive let alone conquer the shadows that besieged my soul. Of all the things that mattered courage was the most important antidote against melancholy it was a way and undoubtedly sweet like satori or a meditation a disconnection from seeing your own ugly image in the mirror.

Poetry was an act a way of forgetting like a one night stand perpetuating forever a glossy nimble rain pouring tellingly crimson sanctified unburdened from the problematic nature of breathing. To believe in tomorrow is essential for overcoming an early death what is there besides hope, and faith? What other power could equate to overcoming the unfortunate stories we delve into those moments staring blank at walls finding inspiration to sooth the melancholy?

What other way is there none I know of, I sought the best books the stories by men who have struggled by men who listened to jazz, and chopin in the quiet. Bliss can be found whenever we sought it out whenever we loosen up drink some beer overcome a demon we have forever put life in a stranglehold. This is where you should begin this is where we all begin.

TASMAN BRIDGE

I see the fog carousing
the skyline over the Tasman
Bridge
I think of Raymond Carver
and what he would've
conjured up
and what simple
metaphor that
would be composed
plain
consumable and
as light as water
and as heavy as
the depths of the human
heart
I watch
and see people in buses and cars
busying themselves
the terror underneath
it all is astounding
nobody wants to admit
it nobody wants to
acknowledge it
they prefer vicariously
living through other people's dreams
of a nobler world
a world without faults, errors

there is no such thing
the only truth is sitting in the storm somewhere being configured
and conjured at this very moment.
finding yourself
knowing yourself is impossible
I've given up trying to understand myself
it's far better to see the music progress
and play;
but a storm can show
remnants of who you could be
maybe it is brighter and clearer than this
river fog

A WAY OUT OF THE MIND

I simply wanted a way to get out of my mind. I was swamped with invisible mangroves that pulsated with my lost emotions and the uncharming desolate waste of my potential.

What was I to be? I felt unwritable; that a part of myself was losing substance, and I didn't know what part of that was. They might as well call it a heart; it's easier to define that part of yourself as the centre of being.

There were a few miserable, dilapidated pine trees outside, a needle in the mind. They lost meaning. Maybe once they stood for something. Well, they obviously stood for life at one point in time in a more merry context. I was being finicky, yet every time I stared out, the more I became lost in my mind.

I couldn't get away from myself; I couldn't accept myself wholly. There was me and the world, my ego, and my potential.

MALTAN SUN

Overrun
with hues of
slow mountainous
cadences
of Mesopotamian
legends sown
into your worsted trench
coat of a desire
to hold the Maltan
sunshine in your veins.

FOUR WALLABIES

As four
wallabies hop
to the rivulet to
drab a drink
from the bowels
of life itself
I am reminded
of how John Keats
reflected on the
nature of the day
to feel your
feet absorb the
way love
stays
when you are
reaching for
something beyond
despair
beyond your ego.

CARE

if you don't
take care of
yourself
the world
will take care
of you in its
own, and that
is the worst.

CHOOSE POETRY

We choose
poetry not
because of the
undertaking
but because
being responsible
for your own heart
is the apotheosis
you deserve

HYMN OF CHRIST

The unfinished
hymn of Jesus Christ
you've got it on your
mind
loving yourself
more than
before
before they made
you fall

AMISS

amiss
the lost kindness
that we found
in grace, I miss
your mossed cheeks
between a brook
and a pomegranate
tree
you wild
spirit of Juniper
fields
I am reborn in a
Tasmanian climate
a sonata
of bone broth
of warmness

FRANKLIN WHARF

It was a grand memory that the shores would leave us remembering the width and shape of the moonlight on that once desolate night rainstorm that ravaged the coastline like Captain Hook would use his hook to rip apart some duvet.

It was amazing the resemblance you had to something I couldn't quite put my finger on. We spent many winters on the beach. We loved the juxtaposition of how the sand felt silky and warm when you buried your head in it. But when the rain came, we'd run back to the shack. to drink tequila. Your neck glowed in the translucence of the moonlight.

Although I am writing from memory, you are the queen of my recollections. The sharpest feeling that I could ever feel It's this silence that creates misery, but you were a chance thought that would bring happiness to life. Your non-existence was even more delightful because I could make you into whatever kind of God I wanted to.

The wharf was fading oak, and as we walked onto the edge and dropped our toes into the water, we stared at the marvel of a storm in the east, and the lighthouse took your attention for a moment. For a moment, I wasn't yours. For a moment, you were someone else's. Even though the lighthouse was inanimate, you seemed to think it was animated with the light reaching the farthest depths of the deep blue. I did value you more than myself. You were a recollection worth valuing.

PINK LEMON

Macabre
pink lemons
on your doorstop
there is a strangeness
to this bliss
everything is out of
place
but not you
you dance
anyway beyond
the peculiarity
of this lucid reverie
of unresolved emotions

FOREVERMORE

Forever opal skin
paralysizing my eyesight
a ill lily floating
on a stagnet
pond in The Tarkine
Rainforest
forever opal skin
parching
a weltering
tone of unremembered
November rainstorms
in Burnie
forever opal skin
something that is
crisper than
my ego
my forever opal skin

BENEATH

Beneath the
symbology
of your consciousness
there were pomegranates
stacked up to the heavens
Japanese Blossoms stamped
to all the raindrops
and you were
without meaning
a detached lullaby
smoked in passion
free of earthly veneer
and you
were impassioned
tolerable
knowledgeable
an avocado tree
bivouacking in a
purple flame

OBSERVATIONAL

It was an observational
error, or maybe it was
that we were lost in the
facade of meaning
what could curtail
the unutterable shadow
of your bosom and to
not waste a moment no
more on what couldn't be
avoided
what if I gave you that fire
it was warm
it was what you wanted
it was inevitable
the convergence of our holiest
conversation it was a set piece
of the heavens the storehouses
of Elohim couldn't stop us from
demanding that the rain arrive
today, and today only and it was
in this proclamation of love that
we were not frayed by fiend that
wanted us to avoid love
and it is your choice to know
the fire it's your choice to
swallow it.

SALESMAN

Onto his second bottle
of wine a vacuum cleaner
salesman has gone into
retirement, he is no longer
wheeling and dealing and
it was nightfall and I'm waiting
for the bus, and the vacuum
salesman has put in his two
week's notice and only works
20 hours a week he is a 42 year
old and is like chinaski chugging
cigarettes down like Fijian water
and I have a chuckle with him
and he says that I don't give a fuck
and that I'm not owned by
any corporation for I'm the salesman
I'm their business
I'm the man who closes deals on
behalf of them and as he is
drinking wine he talks about he is
going to Gold Coast with his
daughter next week and that
he only works for alcohol
and cigarettes and that
he will probably get drunk 4
times a week
and that he is no longer owned

by anyone
as the bus comes I say to him
mate welcome to your retirement
enjoy it
you'll never have to close a deal
again you'll be able to see sun go up

QUESTION

I have
a question
for your soul
will it be
on fire
tomorrow do you know
did you know
I have kept you in
my mind
when nothing is going
right
and that starkly lit
rose on your bedside table
was left by my ribcage
I can't imagine
what you've been
through
only love can imagine
and heal
it

SONGLINE

A few Forester kangaroos
hopped across the road
a rare sight indeed
as they quite athletically
crossed the road
I feel like a young
Henry Lawson
finding the light in
the ridgeways and
the barrenness of
Australia
I saw a wedge tailed eagle
flying onwards to some distant
land, and red hues of forest
gum were knocking on my
eyesight from a distance
and as I leisurely
walked across the road
I saw a few ewes
and a stear galloping in a paddock
filled with testosterone no doubt
I loved seeing farm life
and on occasion I'd whistle
at an emu
and as the sun set its heart
in the distance
Australia isn't just my home

it's my pome
it doesn't matter
where I'm in Australia
I am always connected
to the streams and
trees my Wiradjuri people
were connected to,
I imagine the great Albert Namatjira
dreaming about how he would
paint the Flinders Ranges
and how lifelike
the ranges were
and as I collapse into the songline
of my ancestors
nothing more is real
than the presence of their
spirits on the trails
they once walked
and that a walk about
is the beginning of
knowledge

9.25 AM

It is 9.25 AM
And the sun came out from
the crooked stratus clouds
and on the footpath there was
a lonesome snail trying to
arrive to his destination
and I'm walking around the
carpark writing a poem
and it's Spring and the desolate
mountainous wind is bouncing
of my grey sports coat
and I see a few Jaguars fly past
on the highway and
I see barren carpark
gardens with lifeless ferns
in them and I'm chasing some
dream I don't know about
something elusive
and as I feel the coldness stretch
it's numbing and sharp piercing
stabbing spear onto my shoulders
I want the sun to prance
and any bit of sunlight would
be my friend.

SHE

She couldn't
quite understand
trees she felt as
though they
were misunderstood beings
that their branches
reached beyond
the firmaments
in the sky
she felt as
though they had some
sacred membranous
connection to the
structure and
architecture of being
that if you stood under
a tree and recited a poem
that you'd tap into the
same nature that Whitman
knew from above
and I often repeat Whitman
in my poems for he is a holy
man the christ incarnate
my saviour
and as I write on buses
and jot down notes
of this mysterious woman

that loved trees more than
life itself I feel a strangeness
that I can't explain
it's a feeling that shifts
in the throat momentarily
evidentially it's in these
feelings that words
feel like harps.

MELODY ME

My
passion is
to bend language
like reality and
make melodies
that are completely
unknowable but
that have all the feelings
of life in them

LADY BLACKBIRD

And a lady black bird
broke me and
I got no sincerity only
an ominous taste
from your pink blue corset
and I can't let it go.
I can't let it go.
I am drowning in my own
unreasonableness
I need to love me.
I can't source my old
lyrics that I wrote for church
at the age of sixteen
and today unbroken
I'm unbroken
needing you
to see me
and I'll quarrel with
myself
persecuting myself
and I will
persuade those laurels
to follow me, and they
will be your warden
my lady black bird.

HOBART HYMN

Reflection in
blue silvery ponds
and crestfallen
is the moss on
the boulders
and there was voice
in the crevices
saying love thee
love thee, find what you
lost on the ridgeway
I've could've walked
away feeling unworthy
was it a manifestation
of the Christ? Or was
it me telling me to love
thee, I can't recollect
but that night
Whitman really
showed himself
he showed
what to believe
and that's to be
entangled
in the evermore
verse set in nature
of a Hobart Hymn

ESCAPISM

Escapism is
staring at your own
shadow on the sun-deck
escapism 40 minutes
in the shower with your
own thoughts
escapism is this blank
verse curved in our moment
escapism is us singing
about the moon again
escapism be your
hair touching my eyes
escapism be
our glory
of being in a story
again, again.

IF YOU LOVE

If you love
you've nothing
else to win
nothing else
to prove nothing
else
but
delight
and if your
cat loves you
all the heavens
are yours

PREACHER

The gospel is quite
an undertaking
and there was once
an itinerant preacher
talking about the book of
Isaiah on a lonesome
street behind sodden
marshes and there
were crawdads lazily
sleeping on mangroves
and he had a packet
of marlboro cigarettes
and he spoke of
regret and how finding
the almighty is the
only step, but it's
hard to love your neighbor
all the time, at times war
is the only way to find
grace, and he said if
you loved until the ends
of the earth that Yeshua
would sing you Stairway
to Heaven by Led Zeppelin
and he would take dope with you
and make you part the oceans
but the preacher was

on cocaine you could see
the white powder all
over his fine velvet
red suit jacket.

CLANDESTINE

Clandestine winters
an indefatigable courage
the monstrosity of being
the uncharted fates
the wounds of spring
the angels of behemoth
the legends of evil priests
the purity of the Glasgow sun
the disgrace of death
the blood of unchanging
words the slumber of
night the disquiet of
delight the venerable light
of myths sleeping tight.

ST DAVID'S PARK

And red hues of
moss lined
the pavement of the St David's
Park
and I saw a petite brunette
walking casually reading
Dune by Frank Herbert
and she was cute
and she was trying to forget
the cold of Hobart
the ever changing seasons
and it was overcast
and I wasn't certain that
I would exist anymore
I wanted to be exhumed
gone
I was trying to notice
something that was supposed
to open up
it was supposed to be incisive
and powerful
a spectre spreading its arms
and elbows
against the darkness
that banged against my
trench coat in the unforgiving
wind

in Battery Point
I saw a mulberry
tree scant in fruit
lifeless I scanned for what
remained; a Japanese
Blossom was alive on the edge of
a big hill overlooking
more buildings as I was
walking I kept on thinking
how good it would be
to vanish
to be exhumed
and not alive
like this stone
in Hobart's St David's
Park.
one day that stone
pillar
will be dust
one day I will have no dreams

ELI ELI LAMA SABACHTHANI

Dreamlessly
as I was in paddocks
piled with cadavers
and I was on the side
of the road in a tweed suit
finding misery wherever
I could find it, and many nights
ago the moon was braver than
me, and I was a coward
rotting in a terrifying beautiful
reverie of where we used to
think about our existences
and then it didn't matter
it didn't matter the music
lost its fragrance and stale
toast was more desirable than
fresh rye; and I felt that everything
was tasteless
and as rhythmless, and there
was an insipid waterfall that
was forlorn in my mind; my bowels
are in a state of putrefaction
I was idled in a fire lonesome beyond
what is considered sane
lonesomeness I thought was
a beat designed for a tango with
the sweat of Aphrodite

I don't want to be here anymore
I want to vanish and I am not as
good looking as the moonlight
free of love, and I wanted to weep
like Jesus, but I wasn't up for it.

BOUDOIR

As you walk through
the rain in a bloodstone
orange silk dress I am
reminded of how you
feel like a flute composition
of Wagner, the clouds
are Roseberry, as I imagine
my flesh not locked into
a contract with death
I have found the God in
your breath a sensuous
homestead, boudoir of
silk rose linen sheets
and Italian leather accent
chairs smothered by your
smile.

LAST

What would you do
 if you had one
 kiss left?
could you stomach
that pain could
 you stomach
that? could you believe
in love after death
could you believe in roses
after you see her take her last
breath without
 you?

THANKFUL

Thankful
to have touched
your lips
in the rain
thankful
to have known
how warm your
arms
melting me into
the ground

AUTUMN

I don't want
anything except
the way we rolled
around in the
autumn leaves
those kisses
remain with me
to this very day
do you remember?

UNIVERSE

If she isn't
your flower
you aren't
loving
the universe
right

WILDNESS

She was the wildness
 of the everything you
  desired a tonic
 for everything
  you doubted about
yourself

WHATEVER IT TAKES

doing whatever
it takes is a slippery slope
doing love
now that's more
powerful than doing
whatever it takes

REMEMBER

and as the emptiness of
the sky reminded me of
times sweeter than your
goodbyes I pause
and reflect to deal
with the ordeal of losing
your soul
and they say soul is an overworked
and overused word
I think not
for the word soul fits these lines
perfectly and the word soul
eviscerates everything that stings
and it is sunny and it is Spring
and I lost you
and I know you provided the ink
and I must refuse to give up
fighting and battling against the world
being sick doesn't help but being hard on myself
does not bring you back to life Mum
all I can do is write and not give
up that is all I can do

AMOR

We cannot punctuate
the return of love
nor can we expect it
to happen: many bluebirds
have disappeared this way
through regret
through expectation we
are setting ourselves up
for failure love
is not a promise it's
a happening
it's a refusal of death
it's a dance you won't regret

JAPANESE BLOSSOMS

Japanese white blossoms
keep you awake
nature is an incorruptible
wave of truth
take refuge in
the unanswerable
epigraph of
the nascent
creature of silence
always ebbing always
flowing with the
timeless voice
of love

HONEST

Being honest
with yourself
should be the
religion you die
for

FLOWERS TO GIVE

And it's
the flowers
that gather
the kindness
you need in
order to receive
and give.

LATELY

Lately beloved I've been
too busy worrying about
my own thoughts lately
I've been seclusive
lately I've forgotten
what it means to
be in the sun without
fearing the dark lately
I've been behind the light
lately I've been less myself
less of love lately
I've been a been fading
lately beloved
I have forgotten
what it means to be you
a prayer beyond my own
ego lately.

MOUNT

You desecrate the sweet juicy
mountainous
light with your plush
wine like thighs
and there isn't any imagery
that fits this stable
it's a Sunday morning
and the verses that you
warm with
me accommodate
my bones; come as you
my untouched pine forest
and remnants of your
cowhide full grain coat
are within me shards of an
unknown
quivering Juniper
and you come as are
a piece of strangeness
a valley of wrapped melodies
of rainy glass
stained with
the our truth
 that doesn't
need setting free

NEARLY

nearly
dying this
year in hospital
has taught
me that
loving yourself
in this present moment
is more important
than looking
for the next moment

HAPPENING

I love
you is hard
to say
when you
say it
every fibre
of your being
wants to stay
and they say it's
hard to predict
what's going to happen
next
and being in love
is a continuous
tango of resurrecting
who you need to be
everyday
an apotheosis
a happening
of souls
beginning
again
I know this to be
true
I am a tryer

I don't give up
it's how love
stays

VERSE

writing verse
is a solitary
a godly act
and many are trying
to be the next Byron
or Pessoa
instead of trying to
write lines about
the moon pleasing
your lover's
skin I see a great many
writers yearning
to be the next Bukowski
writing verse is a solitary
act a holy act
a godly
act it must
sync with the
shape of the sunrise
writing verse
shouldn't be terse
it must be well thought out
take a moment
for tomorrow's
verse hasn't arrived
yet it hasn't
become the dance

you need
it happens
when you stop thinking
things will last

JOHN DENVER

John Denver
was born out
of your connexion
to Colorado
lights
and I was drunk last
night thinking of
papyrus snow like
lions singing of Andromeda
and Thespia
was alone on
a brook
and I am gone
in that fold
in that cold.

SOLACE

and idled to your body
was a liquorice shaped
cloud
it was an afterthought
a melody
gratuit
and solaced
by the
velvety green
verdurous pillow
you dreamt of
I was in a trance
an undercurrent
of a Parisian
death

CHASE THE MOON

It wasn't until the haze
cleared that the lovelorn
garlands of our past
appeared
like a hemlock stream
covering our wounds
tumultuous
and vanishing
nothing was left
only the keys you
left under your bed
when you went out
to chase the moon

DAFFODIL

It's good
to be alone
amongst rotten
daffodils
it's good to be
alone
where the
the sting of ocean
air is purer and fair

EAST MOON

The east moon lives in
your skin, and the horizons
live in your feet, and death
lives in your shoulders
you are seeking heaven
a rhapsody of belonging lingers
in your blood your eyes
are love's flood under the veil
of your heartstrings
your sanctity whispers a
curse of your departure
and the sunlight is lost
and love is forevermore
lost in the footprints
of a vanishing shore,
turn your mind to the cold air
that promises the brutal truth
that the universe works for those
who are caught in the frost.

CATS

COPYRIGHT SOURCE LINE ILLEGIBLE

If you love
you've nothing
else to win
nothing else
to prove nothing
else
but
delight
and if your
cat loves you
all the heavens
are yours

WHENEVER

They say it's unhelpful
and pessimistic to
think of death
but death like
life occurs
whenever it
wants to
denying the
thought of death
is a refutation
of life itself

STARK

did you know
I have kept you in
my mind
when nothing is going
right
and that starkly lit
rose on your bedside table
was left by my ribcage
I can't imagine
what you've been
through
only love can imagine
and heal
it

LOVED

And it was
not easy
to love anyone
to love is to redefine
yourself for eternity
there is no
other way to say
it, the miracle of
love is to stay in it
stay the course
and you will meet
the heavens for
the first time.

SELF CARE

And it was
not easy
to love anyone
to love is to redefine
yourself for eternity
there is no
other way to say
it, the miracle of
love is to stay in it
stay the course
and you will meet
the heavens for
the first time.
And it was
not easy
to love anyone
to love is to redefine
yourself for eternity
there is no
other way to say
it, the miracle of
love is to stay in it
stay the course

OCTOBER

It's October and
fourteen weeping,
 unfeeling scarlet myrtles
are carousing the face of
the void it is October and
we are sardonic and chaotic
watching and reminding ourselves
of how to keep happy
when doused in melancholy

STARS

Don't distance
yourself from
the stars in the sky don't
distance yourself from
this melody don't

KNEW

When Whitman touched
my sinew I knew
poetry was worth all
the tears in the world
when Whitman opened
up the world like Tom Waits did
I knew poetry was not only a
duty it is the noblest vocation

GRACE

Every strand
of her hair was
a bluebird singing
under endless moonlight
she was prognostic
and knew the source
of all lyricism
the valley where kisses
where made, and faded

LOVED AND LOVE

Every moment of
love is a religious
event you believe
in it because it
is truer than
all your fears
dear.